The Educational Leader's Guide for School Scheduling

The Educational Leader's Guide for School Scheduling: Strategies Addressing Grades K–12 is the first publication to address creative scheduling at all levels: K–5 or 6, K–8, middle, and high schools. This essential resource provides strategies for the effective and equitable distribution of available FTEs throughout the district, while helping you work through the many critical questions and decisions involved in the scheduling process. Based on the authors' decades of experience in expressing the voice of classroom teachers and building administrators in the art of scheduling, each chapter addresses key schedule development issues, providing a step-by-step sequence, multiple tables, templates, and example schedules. Follow the models in this book to master the skills of producing an efficient organizational plan for your school!

Elliot Y. Merenbloom has been an educational consultant for 24 years. He has served as a classroom teacher, school counselor, assistant principal, principal, director of middle school instruction, and area director in Baltimore County, Maryland.

Barbara A. Kalina has been an educational consultant for over 20 years. She has served as a teacher at Rotolo Middle School Batavia, Illinois and an adjunct professor at Benedictine University and National Louis University.

Other Eye On Education Books
Available from Routledge
(www.routledge.com/eyeoneducation)

The Educational Leader's Guide for School Scheduling

Strategies Addressing Grades K–12

Elliot Y. Merenbloom
Barbara A. Kalina

Routledge
Taylor & Francis Group

NEW YORK AND LONDON

First published 2017
by Routledge
711 Third Avenue, New York, NY 10017

and by Routledge
2 Park Square, Milton Park, Abingdon, Oxon, OX14 4RN

Routledge is an imprint of the Taylor & Francis Group, an informa business

Library of Congress Cataloging-in-Publication Data
A catalog record for this book has been requested

ISBN: 978-1-138-20739-4 (hbk)
ISBN: 978-1-138-20742-4 (pbk)
ISBN: 978-1-315-46233-2 (ebk)

Typeset in Optima
by Apex CoVantage, LLC

Contents

Detailed Contents

Tables

Meet the Authors

Elliot Y. Merenbloom

Prior to Elliot Y. Merenbloom's 24-year career as an educational consultant, he served in the Baltimore County (Maryland) Public Schools as a classroom teacher, school counselor, assistant principal, principal, director of middle school instruction, and area director.

A graduate of Towson University (undergraduate) and Loyola University Maryland (Master's of Education and Advanced Certificate in Education), his areas of expertise include creative scheduling, restructuring schools in the change process, teaching strategies for variable-length time periods, and implementing team/small learning community approaches to instruction.

He conducted workshops for the American Association for School Administrators, Association for Supervision and Curriculum Development, National Association of Secondary School Principals, and Association for Middle Level Education (AMLE). He served as a consultant for school districts in 45 states as well as Guam; Vienna, Austria; and Vancouver, BC.

Barbara A. Kalina

Barbara A. Kalina holds both bachelor's and master's degrees from Mundelein College in Chicago, IL. Besides her 23 years in the classroom, Barbara served on the Illinois State Board of Education Language Arts Committee, as adjunct professor at Benedictine University and National Louis University, each in Illinois, and as an educational consultant for more than 20 years as well as a board member of the Association of Illinois Middle-Grade Schools.

Barbara conducts workshops in and presents nationally on research-based literacy strategies, teaching strategies for effective use of a master schedule, and middle school philosophy implementation as well as teaming/small learning community organization.

A long-standing member of and conference presenter with the Association of Illinois Middle-Grade Schools, Association for Middle-Level Education, Association for Supervision and Curriculum Development, Illinois Association for Supervision and Curriculum Development, and Learning Forward, formerly the National Staff Development Council, she has written numerous educational articles on instruction and effective use of time within the schedule.

Collaborative Publications and Webinar

Elliot Y. Merenbloom and Barbara A. Kalina co-authored *Making Creative Schedules Work in Middle and High Schools* (2007) and *Creative Scheduling for Diverse Populations in Middle and High School: Maximizing Opportunities for Learning* (2012), both books published by Corwin Press.

Recently, Elliot Y. Merenbloom and Barbara A. Kalina collaborated on an entry in *The Encyclopedia of Middle Grades Education* published by Information Age (2016) entitled *Scheduling: Creating Flexible Interdisciplinary Blocks of Time*. They also co-wrote *Scheduling Time for Interdisciplinary Collaboration*, May 2015 in the *AMLE* magazine, a publication of the Association for Middle Level Education, and presented an AMLE Webinar addressing the joint collaboration of the administrator's voice and the teacher's voice in the scheduling process.

Preface

In 1991, an administrator and a teacher met at a National Middle School Association workshop. Discovering that they shared a common vision for education, they began to provide the voice of the administrator and the voice of the teacher to other administrators and teachers. The administrator, Elliot Y. Merenbloom, and the teacher, Barbara A. Kalina, designed efficient and equitable schedules. To implement the schedules, they developed a research-based instructional method to unlock the potential of the schedule in enhancing student achievement.

Their publications and presentations address the many variations of grade configurations within schools: K–5 or 6, K–8, middle, and high schools. Collaboratively, they share insights and knowledge with the educational community through two earlier books, multiple articles, and an entry in *The Encyclopedia of Middle Grades Education* as well as presentations at multiple professional conferences and individual school/district work.

Believing that anything affecting student needs should be a shared process, Elliot and Barbara encourage shared responsibility between the superintendent and other educational leaders in schedule development. Although scheduling requires acquaintance with a definite skill set, they realize that prospective administrators and instructional supervisors rarely receive training in their graduate courses to provide those skills.

A void seems to exist in addressing the comprehensive scheduling needs of K–12 grade levels. This book addresses the scheduling process for all levels K–12, including scheduling for the K–8 school, emphasizing the need for fluidity in the process.

Chapter Organization

Each chapter in this book addresses questions that are or should be formed by any person or group attempting to develop an educational schedule. Following is a synopsis of each chapter and its fit in the scheduling process.

Chapter 1 Schedules: Achieving Efficiency and Equity

- Defining efficiency and equity

- Strategies to achieve efficiency and equity

- Roles and responsibilities of stakeholders

Chapter 2 Core Elements in the Development of a School Schedule: District and School Perspectives

- Essential elements and specific language of scheduling

- Importance of mission/vision statement

- Schedules, curriculum, and diverse populations

- Providing avenues for Response to Intervention

- Consideration of organizational options

- Impact of teachers' contracts

- Small learning communities

- Flexibility

- Least restrictive environment

- Financial resources

- Credit recovery

- CTE and other alternatives

- Schedule implementation

Chapter 3 Managerial Strategies

- Tally
- Department summary
- FTE distribution chart
- Teacher assignment chart
- Conflict matrix
- Blueprint

Chapter 4 Organizational Frameworks

- Primary options K–12
- Inserts K–12

Chapter 5 Steps in Building a K–5 or K–6 Schedule

- Steps to create schedule
- Tables illustrating specific steps

Chapter 6 Steps in Building a K–8 Schedule

- Steps to create schedule
- Tables illustrating specific steps

Chapter 7 Steps in Building a Middle School Schedule

- Steps to create schedule
- Tables illustrating specific steps

Chapter 8 Steps in Building a High School Schedule

- Steps to create schedule
- Tables illustrating specific steps

Chapter 9 Aspects of Schedule Implementation

- Computer usage
- Establishing goals
- Professional development
- Common planning time
- Lesson planning

Special Features

Multiple tables within the scheduling chapters provide visual images of the recommended steps. Selected tables will be available online so readers can print and use them in their own contexts.

Each chapter concludes with "Recap" and "Points to Consider" sections.

Applications

Finally, how this book is used by the educational community will affect schedule development at many levels. As a text for graduate courses, it will prepare educational leaders to develop or oversee the development of schedules. Within districts, the book becomes a handbook for training prospective educational leaders and for each school to evaluate and guide the scheduling process. Ultimately, the book emphasizes the importance of a school schedule in providing effective instruction and to enable the stakeholders and community to recognize that the schedule is not an end in itself but a means to that goal.

Acknowledgment

Elliot Y. Merenbloom and Barbara A. Kalina wish to thank Ilene Merenbloom, Rebecca Collazo, Kate Fornadel and Heather Jarrow at Routledge for their invaluable support in the preparation of this manuscript.

eResources

Keep an eye out for the eResources icon throughout this book, which indicates a resource is available online. Resources mentioned in this book can be downloaded, printed, used to copy/paste text, and/or manipulated to suit your individualized use. You can access these downloads by visiting the book product page on our website:

www.routledge.com/products/9781138207424

Then click on the tab that reads "eResources" and then select the file(s) you need. The file(s) will download directly to your computer.

Schedules
Achieving Efficiency and Equity

Focus

- Defining efficiency and equity
- Strategies to achieve efficiency and equity
- Roles and responsibility of stakeholders

Well-developed schedules contain ingredients for well-run schools and well-delivered curriculum. Unfortunately, schedule developers do not universally understand or efficiently construct master schedules. Well-constructed schedules fulfill specific criteria discussed in this chapter with the recommendation that specific stakeholders are involved.

A successful schedule provides a vehicle to meet the mission/vision statement of the school or district. Mission/vision statements provide guidelines for all school-related decisions that involve schedules as well as curriculum, strategies, and services. In its active form, the schedule graphically represents the core values of a school. Not an end in itself, the schedule provides the means to the end of delivering required and elective curriculum to all students, including diverse subsets of the student population. In essence, schedules fulfill the mission/vision statement or confirm the need to update or expand the statement.

The structure of the schedule provides the order of the day for teachers and students. Because the organizational plan maximizes the contribution of all full-time equivalent (FTE) staff members, input from that group as well as all constituency groups becomes an important ingredient in schedule development. Further, the well developed schedule provides a comprehensive structure to honor course requests of all students.

An Efficient Schedule Defined

Building principals have primary responsibility for creating an efficient schedule. A principal who sees the big picture of a school as well as subsets or parts of that picture should lead the design of the schedule. As the instructional leader, the principal is most aware of the comprehensive student population, its diversity, the expertise and tenure of the staff, and expectations of the community. Fulfilling the mission/ vision statement, the principal and scheduling team seek a schedule that focuses on student learning. In that regard, current research and best practices that enhance the teaching/learning process bring teachers into this exploration phase.

An efficient schedule makes the best use of all FTE positions and takes into account variances that may occur from the mean average daily pupil loads of those teachers. Rather than guess at possible influential data, decisions on FTE use and assignment must be based on data that are solid and available.

Student needs also must be considered with hard data. Through the use of hard data, the efficient schedule provides the highest percentage of students with their first choice of required courses and electives. By providing a blend of first choice courses and electives, the schedule becomes a catalyst to move students toward college and career readiness. In addition, student mobility rates affect academic success and need consideration. This factor may present one of the more difficult issues in developing an efficient schedule.

Further, the schedule sets the stage for meaningful instruction. The allotted class time should maximize meaningful instruction that promotes personalization and opportunities for the integration of curriculum content and skills. Besides class time, teacher collaboration time appears in schedules. Another important factor is the minimization of time lost by staff due to travel between schools. Finally, the efficient schedule is not etched in stone but adds efficiency because of its adaptability when future needs warrant modification or expansion.

Responsibility for efficiency, however, is not just the task of principals. Superintendents lead by setting the tone, collaborating with principals, and monitoring the extent to which all schools are efficient within available resources.

An Equitable Schedule Defined

An equitable schedule influences and honors the teachers' contract and allocates responsibilities equally and respectfully among all staff members. A part of equity resides in routine monitoring by the central office for the distribution of available FTEs throughout the district as well as within each school.

Student needs influence the construction of an equitable schedule. Attending to the diverse needs of students individually, in cohort groups, and at different grade levels, the schedule may vary according to those grade levels. Meeting secondary school student requests becomes as vital for their personalized education as meeting their learning needs. K–5, K–6, and K–8 schools should provide both similar and special programs for all students. At all levels, the equitable schedule provides opportunities for enrichment and remediation as complements to the curriculum and a least restrictive environment for all students.

Roles of Stakeholders

Superintendent and Central Office Personnel

A major goal of schedule development is to provide a constructive vehicle to establish a school system and not a system of schools. The superintendent and central office personnel orchestrate and assess the organization and scheduling process throughout the school system. In their assessment, they monitor equity in distribution of school-based and support personnel in relation to student needs throughout the district. They coordinate the role of the business/finance and curriculum departments to offer input as needed or requested. In their assessments and monitoring, they demonstrate fiscal responsibility to the board of education and the community.

Principal

By focusing on a specific school, the principal uses department summaries objectively and critically to make decisions on the distribution of staff assignments. Prior to firm schedule decisions, the principal evaluates the considered primary framework(s) and inserts in light of staff readiness to implement the schedule. Vital in this process, professional development allows teachers to assume ownership of the schedule and its implementation. A mistake would be to end the schedule developmental process prior to professional development and assume implementation would continue unflawed. Rather, supervision and assessment of instructional time use allotted in the schedule needs to be ongoing.

School Counselors

The school counselor's role varies widely from school to school and district to district. Consequently, the counselor's role needs to be clearly defined. Often, counselors are given total responsibility for organizing the school rather than providing input about the schedule to benefit the students they serve. While part of their role can be that of assisting in building the schedule, they should not be totally responsible for the administrative decisions necessary for schedule development, including FTE distribution. While they can assist in analyzing the various iterations of the schedule as it is being developed, their main responsibility lies in helping students with course selection and working through irresolvable conflicts until all students are fully scheduled. From the initial registration process through the summer and the entire school year, their expertise and input on behalf of students is vital.

Teachers

In order for the schedule to be implemented efficiently and equitably, teachers are an essential part of the scheduling committee. Their input aids decision-making such as schedule organization and the recommendation for courses that address the needs of diverse students, such as honors, dual enrollment, and Tier 3. Teachers' expertise enables programs such as magnets, pathways, small learning communities, and professional learning communities to be established appropriately within the schedule. By the same token, teachers need opportunities for professional development to effectively implement the schedule and maintain the integrity of collaboration time.

Achieving Flexibility Within Structure

In today's society and culture, an efficient and equitable school schedule mandates organization and structure. The community demands structure for the safety and education of its children. Further, both teachers and students require a defined timetable of classes and responsibilities. To achieve these ends, numerous structural options are available at the elementary, middle, and high school levels.

Within defined structures, opportunities for flexibility can be created. In some cases, a cohort or team of teachers manages flexibility; in other cases, principals and central office personnel encourage teachers to be flexible, creative, and innovative in their classroom instruction.

Because correlation exists between how time is used and student achievement, the most efficient and equitable schedules encourage teachers to make creative uses of time. Therefore, structure is the prerequisite for the existence of flexibility, requiring professional development as the catalyst to achieve flexibility in grades K–12.

Recap

Educational leaders are responsible for efficient and equitable schedules from district and individual school perspectives. They have complementary and collaborative responsibilities toward this end. The next chapter introduces a common scheduling language for all stakeholders.

Points to Consider

1. Is the topic of school organization/scheduling approached at the district as well as the school level?

2. How are responsibilities for specific phases of the scheduling process developed at each level of schooling?

3. Is the mission/vision statement a guide for scheduling?

4. How are the diverse needs of all students considered?

5. In what ways do hard data influence decisions about FTE distribution, course offerings, and instructional time?

6. How are structure and flexibility related or interrelated?

7. At the school level, how are principals, teachers, and counselors involved in developing and assessing the schedule?

8. How is the community informed of aspects of scheduling/organization?

Core Elements in the Development of a School Schedule
District and School Perspectives

Focus

- Essential elements and specific language of scheduling
- Schedules, curriculum, and diverse populations
- Consideration of organizational options
- Impact of teachers' contracts
- Small learning communities

Elements and vocabulary in this chapter serve as the foundation for creating efficient and equitable schedules across grades K–12. An enumeration of core elements with explanations appears. School and district stakeholders along with committee members apply this knowledge to establish goals that guide the process.

Mission/Vision

As indicated in Chapter 1, the mission/vision statement of the district as well as the school needs to guide decisions. The statement serves as a foundation for determining the direction of decisions to be made.

Consequently, the schedule becomes the action plan to achieve the goals described in the mission/vision statement.

Delivering the Curriculum

Schedules are a means to an end, not an end unto themselves. The desired end is to deliver a curriculum that meets student needs and course requests. School schedules cannot be designed until curriculum offerings are in place and known to all stakeholders, including students.

Diverse Populations

Diversity appears in the complex fabric of schools as well as society. Today's awareness and acceptance of the rich embroidery of beliefs, personalities, and abilities challenge schools to find equitable ways to provide for diversity. The schedule provides a pathway to meet those demands by accommodating multiple programs designed to meet the needs of all students.

Equity and efficiency of the schedule are major factors in determining whether all students have access to a full spectrum of courses and opportunities. Essential programs for a diverse student body need to fit under the single umbrella of the schedule designed. Meanwhile, the school and district should monitor the patterns of new student entries and withdrawals.

Response to Intervention

Depending on the interpretation and needs for intervention, Response to Intervention (RtI) practices differ from district to district. Prior to the meeting of the school scheduling committee, the district has an agreed understanding of RtI implementation as well as definition of each tier. At all levels, an efficient schedule provides fluidity between the tiers and opportunities for teacher collaboration to manage student assignment to the tiers.

Elementary

Some schools include an intervention team and schedule it as a key component in the development of a blueprint for their schedule. The research of Howell, Patton, and Deiote (2008) reveals that students who are two or more years behind their peers fail to catch up without intervention. Focusing on that research, schools with successful RtI programs begin frequent, intense, and durable interventions from first grade, often with an intervention team to supplement the efforts of the grade-level classroom teacher.

Middle School

Efficient use of instructional time that exists in a fixed or flexible schedule best addresses Tier 1 interventions. Use of articulated engagements within that time encourages depth of understanding. Further, strategic use of differentiated strategies meets the needs of several tiers during the regularly scheduled time.

Tier 2 interventions can be delivered through a flex/advisory/intervention period within the schedule. These interventions are typically operated or coordinated by an interdisciplinary team. In addition to the use of the flex/advisory/intervention period, Tier 3 interventions sometimes appear within the exploratory/elective portion of the schedule. This approach, however, denies the student full participation in the total curriculum offered by the school.

High School

Efficient use of instructional time meets the needs of Tier 1 interventions. Because a risk of losing credits exists when students are assigned intervention classes, Tier 2 interventions are best achieved within a freshman academy, house, or small learning community. The more complex and intense Tier 3 interventions may be schedu! J as a course.

Organizational Frameworks: Primary and Inserts

Scheduling options should be known by all district ar J school-based personnel. As choices narrow, the district office stafi confirms the primary frameworks and inserts to be considered at eac school. Regardless of the organizational frameworks chosen, proi ssional development for all teachers is essential in order for effective mple-mentation to occur.

Primary Frameworks

Typically, elementary schools employ a modular version of a trad tional schedule in which a single module equals the amount of time allocated for art, music, and/or physical education. Generally, English/language arts and math are scheduled for double modules. Middle schools employ traditional or day 1/day 2 primary frameworks while K–8 schools use a combination of the modular version of a traditional schedule in the elementary grades and traditional or day 1/day 2 schedules in grades 6, 7, and 8. High schools select from more options: semester 1/semester 2, day 1/day 2, traditional, or trimester frameworks.

Inserts

Insert options include double English/double math, single-subject teams, combination teams, interdisciplinary-maximum flexibility, inter-disciplinary-limited flexibility, interdisciplinary-exploratory/elective, credit recovery, and rotational schedule. All of the inserts can be scheduled in any of the primary schedules. A number of the options enable flexibility within the schedule.

 ## Teachers' Contracts

Multiple factors beyond the curriculum influence the schedule. Teachers' contracts must be honored. The percent of time that teachers have student contact affects the FTE needed. While collaboration time needs to exist within the schedule, how that time is used must be mutually understood while acknowledging who owns that time. The length of the teacher's lunch may impact the number of instructional minutes available. Further, the length of the school day affects the number and length of instructional modules. Traveling teachers influence the effective use of FTEs. Finally, who has a vote in the final schedule form: board of education members, teachers, other stakeholders?

 ## Small Learning Communities

Multiple forms of small learning communities exist at all levels. These communities aid teachers in responding to student needs and data, discussing teaching strategies, personalizing the learning experience, integrating the curriculum, and exploring opportunities for flexibility. Consequently, successful schedule builders include opportunities for common planning time to support the small learning communities. In order to maximize the impact of common planning time, teacher training is essential.

 ## Flexibility

Structure sets the stage for flexibility. If implemented well, it allows for a greater response to student needs and gives teachers either in cohort groups or individually the ability to control time (Sousa, 2001, p. 101,

Sylwester, 1995). One format for flexibility lies in a flex/advisory/intervention period that exists within certain framework

Least Restrictive Environment

The requirement for providing the least restrictive environment for all students does not pertain only to special education or English language learner (ELL) students. The equitable schedule guarantees student participation in all aspects of the curriculum. As Robert Marzano (2003, p.22.) recommends, all students deserve the "opportunity to learn." Therefore, schedules should be individualized at the various school levels. Effort must be made in scheduling exploratory/elective classes to accommodate special education students as well as those who need Tier 3 of RtI. Further, when writing Individualized Education Programs (IEPs), the realities of the school schedule must be considered.

Financial Resources

The efficiency of a schedule directly relates to resources available at the district level. Superintendents distribute FTEs to each school. The distribution of FTEs within the schools, however, rests with the principal and the leadership team. The school leadership team oversees equitable distribution of FTE among departments and grade levels, basing those decisions on student requests, needs, and enrollment.

Credit Recovery

Credit recovery may be a key factor in increasing graduation rates. While many districts use software packages to aid students in recovering credit, a lack of consistency and unequal presentation of curriculum reveals their use to be less effective than teacher-led instruction.

Accommodating CTE and Other Alternatives

Location for the delivery of programs and core courses for career and technology education (CTE) pathways varies. Sometimes they can be offered in the home building, but often they are travel programs to a central location. Travel times must sync with the home school schedule to avoid a loss of credit due to travel time. A day 1/day 2 schedule allows students to attend the home school on one day and the CTE center on the other day. Since first introduced into the educational scene, the changing focus of CTE integrates skills and content in light of career opportunities.

Schedule Implementation

Open and effective communication with all stakeholders becomes the vital ingredient for implementation with the superintendent and principal overseeing the initial presentation and the ongoing evaluation of the new schedule. Through professional development sessions, teachers need to assume ownership of the new schedule so that they can adequately implement it and aid in explaining it to the board of education and the community.

Recap

This chapter defines key terms or concepts used in the development of efficient and equitable school schedules. Effective educational leaders understand these terms and concepts as well as recognize that the schedule is a means to deliver the curriculum to a diverse student population. School and district stakeholders along with committee members apply this knowledge to establish goals that guide the process. Chapter 3 presents a set of managerial strategies to achieve an efficient and equitable schedule.

Points to Consider

1. How do the chosen frameworks accommodate the district's curriculum?

2. What diversity issues must be factored into a new schedule?

3. How will the schedule include our RtI program?

4. What organizational frameworks best fit our student and curricular needs?

5. How will the teachers' contract influence the schedule?

6. How are the needs of small learning communities met in the schedule?

7. How can the schedule design provide opportunities for flexibility?

8. How does the schedule provide all students with equal opportunities to learn?

9. How does FTE allocation affect the schedule?

10. How have the district's finances impacted the schedule?

Works Cited

Howell, R. J., Patton, S. L., Deiotte, M. T. (2008). *Understanding response to intervention: A practical guide to systemic implementation*. Bloomington, IN: Solution Tree.

Marzano, R. J. (2003). *What works in schools: Translating research into action*. Alexandria, VA: Association for Supervision and Curriculum Development.

Sousa, D. A. (2001). *How the brain learns: A classroom teacher's guide*. Thousand Oaks, CA: Corwin Press.

Sylwester, R. (1995). *A celebration of neurons: An educator's guide to the human brain*. Alexandria, VA: Association for Supervision and Curriculum Development.

Managerial Strategies

 ## Focus

- Tally
- Department summary
- FTE distribution chart
- Teacher assignment chart
- Conflict matrix
- Blueprint

Managerial strategies aid the efficient and equitable distribution of available resources throughout the district as well as the school. They ensure consistency in meeting the needs of a diverse population. Based on student enrollment and course requests, these strategies increase the likelihood of secondary students receiving their first choice of courses. All of the listed strategies precede the actual creation of the master schedule. Visual examples illustrate each strategy.

 ## Tally

The tally summarizes the number of students in an elementary or middle school grade as well as the number of secondary students who request a specific course in each department.

Table 3.1 Elementary Tally

Grade	Enrollment	Sections	Average Class Size
K	127	5	25.4
1	136	5	27.2
2	118	5	23.6
3	140	6	23.3
4	151	6	25.2
5	127	5	25.4

The middle school example shows potential core sections and team structures. Additionally, students may have opportunities for electives in grades 5–8.

Table 3.2 Middle School Tally to Determine Sections and Team Structures

Grade	Enrollment	Sections	Average Class Size	Potential Team Structure(s)
5	100	4	25	2,2 4
6	130	6	21.6	2,2,2 3,3 4,2
7	200	8	25	4,4
8	250	10	25	5,5

At the high school level, the tally reflects the enrollment in required courses and requests for electives. It is the basis of the department summary and, ultimately, the number of FTE teachers in each department.

The high school example represents a segment of a total department summary. Because co-taught (CT) Algebra I and co-taught (CT) Geometry students are included in the number of requests, those numbers are in parentheses. The identification of the number of courses that will have CT students aids the departmental assignment of special education teachers who will co-teach. Including the date on the tally

Table 3.3 High School Tally: Mathematics. March 1, 2017

Course	Requests	Sections	Average Class Size
H Algebra I	53	2	26.5
Algebra I	93	4	23.3
CT Algebra I	16	(3)	(5.3)
H Geometry	112	4	28.0
Geometry	200	8	25.0
CT Geometry	36	(5)	(7.2)

allows for change to occur between the original registration and the opening of school. Students may not meet the prerequisites of a particular course, require a schedule modification due to an updated IEP, or change their elective courses.

Department Summary

Determining equitable distribution of FTEs in light of course requests may be the single most important managerial strategy in secondary schools. Primarily a high school strategy, it may be needed in middle schools if the exploratory/electives portion of the schedule is highly individualized or core courses are leveled. The previously completed tally is entered in the "enrollment" column of the summary.

Table 3.4 Sample Mathematics Department Summary

Course	Enrollment	Sections	Average Class Size	Weight	Aggregate Periods
H Algebra I	53	2	26.5	5	10
Algebra I	93	4	23.3	5	20
CT Algebra	16	(3)	(5.3)	—	—
H Geometry	112	4	28	5	20
Geometry	200	8	25	5	40
CT Geometry	36	(5)	(7.2)	—	—

Continued

Table 3.4 Continued

Course	Enrollment	Sections	Average Class Size	Weight	Aggregate Periods
Tier 3 Math	46	7	6.6	2.5	17.5
H Algebra II	100	4	25	5	20
Algebra II	215	9	23.9	5	45
CT Algebra II	50	(9)	(5.5)	–	–
Total					**172.5**
					Divided by 30 = 5.75 teachers
					Divided by 25 = 6.9 teachers

Explanation of Table Columns

- The sections column is based on the desired average class s ⸱ for each course in light of student course requests and FTEs avai ⸱le. As previously presented, the CT sections are included withi he regular course enrollment figures.

- Average class size is an important indicator in light of teach ⸱ contracts in the event a section needs to be deleted or added in t final analysis of the department or school.

- Weight represents the valence or relative time value of a course. For instance, a course that meets five times a week for the year receives a weight of 5. Courses that meet every other day for the year or every day for a semester receive a weight of 2.5. Courses that meet the equivalent of 2 periods per day for the year receive a weight of 10.

- Aggregate periods of instruction are the total amount of teaching time needed for that course. To determine the aggregate periods per course, multiply the number of sections by the weight of the course.

● FTE required for that department arises from the total aggregate periods or amount of teaching time for that department divided by the number of periods per week that a teacher can teach. A higher number of periods per week that a teacher can teach results in a lower number of teachers needed in that department.

FTE Distribution Chart

After calculating the total number of teachers desired for each department, the FTE request must conform to the total allocated by the superintendent. The chart reflects equitable distribution among departments. If the total number requested exceeds the allotment, a reduction is needed. Reductions are accomplished by identifying courses with the lowest average class size and reducing the number of sections when possible. Occasionally, a high school elective may need to be dropped.

Table 3.5 Sample High School FTE Distribution Chart

Department	FTE Requested
English	9.5
Social Studies	8.0
Mathematics	10.0
Science	9.0
World Language	6.0
Business	4.5
Physical Education	4.75
Art	3.0
Music	3.0
Agriculture	2.7
Total	**60.45**

In middle schools, the distribution chart monitors enrollment or average class size in exploratory/elective courses. Elementary school principals should monitor the balance between class size in core and specials classes. Lower average class size in core classes may result in less availability of specials teachers or higher class si   in specials classes. Availability of specials teachers is a factor in setting the stage for collaboration.

Teacher Assignment Chart

After the FTE distribution chart is approved, teacher assignmen s begin. In the secondary grades, the average daily student loads of achers are monitored to achieve equity. Table 3.6 illustrates two scena ios for teaching periods: 25 and 30 periods per week.

Table 3.6 Sample Teacher Assignment Chart

Department	Teacher	Assignment	Aggregate Periods	Student Lo
Mathematics	John Ward	4 Algebra I	20	126
		1 H Algebra I	5	
			Total 25	
	Kristine Bolster	4 Tier 3 Math	10	150
		2 H Algebra I	10	
		2 CT Algebra II	10	
			Total 30	

Conflict Matrix

Critical in identifying the pattern of students' course requests and separate from the compilation of course tallies, the conflict matrix maximizes the likelihood of students receiving the first choice of courses. Language to understand course distribution within the schedule follows:

- A singleton course refers to a course with only one section. To minimize conflicts, place these courses in different periods of the school day and schedule them first.

- Doubletons refer to courses with two sections. These also need to be spread accordingly.

In the following table, a critical analysis identifies patterns of student course requests. Based on data from the department summary, the spread of singletons and doubletons becomes the focus for this matrix.

Table 3.7 Portion of Conflict Matrix for Honors English 11

Course	Enrollment	Potential Sections
H English 11	27	1
H American History	24	1
American History	3	7
H Geometry	22	1
Geometry	5	6
Probability and Statistics	8	1
H Physics	20	1
Physics	7	4
French III	27	1

- Twenty-seven students enrolled in Honors English 11. Of this group, 24 selected Honors American History while the remaining 3 selected standard American History, which has seven sections. The Honors English 11 and Honors American History singleton courses need to be placed in different periods.

- Of the 27 students in Honors English 11, 22 are in Honors Geometry while 5 are in standard Geometry, a six-section course. Additionally, 8 of the 27 enrolled in the singleton Probability and Statistics course, requiring the sections to be scheduled in different periods.

- Of the 27 students in Honors English 11, 20 enrolled in Honors Physics while 7 opted for standard Physics, a four-section course. Honors Physics needs to be placed in a different period than Honors English 11, Honors American History, Honors Geometry, and Probability and Statistics.

- All 27 students enrolled in French III. This course is placed in a period different from the other singletons.

Table 3.8 Placing Singletons in the Master Schedule

Period	1	2	3	4	5	6	7	8
Course	H English 11	H American History	H Physics		H Geom- etry	Proba- bility & Statistics	French III	Band/ Chorus

In the middle grades, visual monitoring accommodate individ-ualized scheduling within core or exploratory/elective portions of the schedule. Using this process, schedulers place a student properly in core as well as exploratory/elective classes.

Table 3.9 Middle School Interdisciplinary Team

Subject	1	2	3	4	5	6	7	8	9
English	H 8–01	CT 8–01	CT 8–02	Team Meeting	Plan	Lunch	8–03	8–04	8
Social Studies	8–01	8–02	8–03	Team Meeting	Plan	Lunch	8–04	8–05	8–0
Math	8–01	H 8–01	H 8–02	Team Meeting	Plan	Lunch	CT 8–02	CT 8–03	8–04
Science	8–01	8–02	8–03	Team Meeting	Plan	Lunch	8–04	8–05	8–06
Special Educa-tion		CT English	CT English	Team Meeting	Plan	Lunch	CT Math	CT Math	

Blueprint

The preliminary draft or design of the master schedule, blueprints are essential at the elementary and middle school levels as well as high schools with freshman academies or small learning communities. In the middle grades, the blueprint reflects the placement of exploratory/

elective classes and becomes a visual guide for extended-time classes. If the school has an intervention team, those classes can be placed in the blueprint as well.

Table 3.10 Middle School Blueprint

Period	Grade 6	Grade 7	Grade 8
1	Core	Core	Exploratory/Electives
2	Core	Core	Exploratory/Electives
3	Core	Core	Intervention
4	Lunch	Intervention	Core
5	Intervention	Lunch	Core
6	Core	Exploratory/Electives	Lunch
7	Core	Exploratory/Electives	Core
8	Exploratory/Electives	Core	Core
9	Exploratory/Electives	Core	Core

Recap

Strategies in this chapter maximize the contribution of all available FTEs in the district in an efficient and equitable way. The ultimate responsibility for this distribution among all schools lies with the superintendent. Building principals distribute assigned FTEs among departments and grade levels with an eye toward efficiency and equity. Organizational structures and illustration, the remaining pieces of background information, appear in Chapter 4.

Points to Consider

1. What professional development is in place for central office and school-based personnel to learn the managerial strategies?

2. How does the superintendent monitor consistent use of managerial strategies?

3. How does the building principal monitor consistent use of managerial strategies?

4. What does the scheduling committee learn from the tally of course requests?

5. What can the scheduling committee learn from the department summaries and FTE distribution chart?

6. What issues arise in the conflict matrix chart?

7. How does the blueprint enhance extended-time core periods

Organizational Frameworks

Focus

- Frameworks K–12
- Primary options
- Inserts

Needs of districts and schools require personalized development of schedules. Consequently, framework variety offers opportunities for schedule builders to meet those needs. Primary frameworks remain fixed and allow inserts to provide flexibility within the schedule. Regardless of the frameworks chosen, curriculum implications exist, including professional development needed to connect the schedule with the teaching/learning process.

Primary

The primary scheduling choice forms the overall structure and provides the basis of the major design of the master schedule. In essence, the principal controls movement and sequence in this schedule in which all classes begin and end at the same time. To provide school-specific schedules, any of the primary schedules can include or house any of the inserts.

Traditional

In secondary schools, traditional schedules can be 6, 7, 8, or 9 periods typically made up of 40–50-minute classes. At the elementary or K–8 levels, a modular schedule is used. Based on the length of the school day and the teachers' contract, the school day can be subdivided into 7–12 modules ranging from 35–50 minutes per module. Lunch appears as a full period or module. Numerous inserts can be applied to create a schedule distinctive to the district or school.

As noted in Table 4.1, the teachers' contract influences the number of periods or modules and efficiency of the teacher workday.

Table 4.1 Efficiency of Teacher Workday

6-Period Day	7-Period Day	8-Period Day	9-Period Day	Period Day
5/6 = 83%	5/7 = 71%	5/8 = 63%	5/9 = 55%	5/10 = 50%
	6/7 = 86%	6/8 = 75%	6/9 = 67%	6/10 = 60%
		7/8 = 87%	7/9 = 78%	7/10 = 70%
			8/9 = 89%	8/10 = 80%
				9/10 = 90%

Significant financial and scheduling implications exist as a result of the teachers' contract. If teachers have but one planning period, collaboration or common planning time is jeopardized; therefore the preservation of common planning time requires effort and vision and, subsequently, efficient and effective use by teachers.

Semester 1/Semester 2

Typically presented as a high school model, the semester 1/semester 2 schedule primarily exists to maximize instructional time. Bells ring at fixed times, but inserts can override the bells. In this schedule, the student focuses on fewer classes at a time and a teacher is responsible for three sections per semester.

Table 4.2 Elementary School
Teacher Modular Schedule

Mod	Assignment
1	Reading/Language Arts
2	
3	
4	Social Studies
5	Lunch/Recess
6	Mathematics
7	
8	Science
9	Planning
10	Intervention

Table 4.3 Middle School Teacher
Traditional Schedule

Period	Class
1	English 8–01
2	English 8–02
3	Team meeting
4	Personal Plan
5	Lunch
6	H-English 8–01
7	English 8–03
8	English 8–04
9	Intervention

Table 4.4 High School Student Traditional Schedule

Period	Class
1	English
2	World Cultures
3	Biology
4	Biology Lab/Physical Education
5	Lunch
6	Geometry
7	Spanish II
8	Flex/Advisory/Intervention
9	Band

The schedule presents an 8-period day excluding lunch, which is generally a module of time within periods 3 and 7. In the first semester, periods 1–4 are scheduled at 90 minutes each; in the second semester periods 5–8 are scheduled at 90 minutes each. Periods 3 and 7 are extended by 30 minutes for lunch. For effe ive instruction within these longer time periods, professional develof nent reinforces the abilities of teachers to use a pacing guide and active engagement models.

Table 4.5 Semester 1/Semester 2 Teacher Schedu e

Semester 1			Semester 2	
Period	Course		Period	Cour e
1	H-Geometry 01		5	H-Alg bra II 01
2	Plan		6	Plan
3	Geometry 01		7	Algebra I 01
4	Geometry 02		8	Geometı 03

Table 4.6 Semester 1/Semester 2 High School Student Schedule

Semester 1			Semester 2	
Period	Course		Period	Course
1	H-English 11		5	Pre-Calculus
2	US History		6	Chemistry
3	Band		7	Band
4	Spanish III		8	Physical Education

Day 1/Day 2

Regarded as an effort to maximize instructional time, the day 1/day 2 master schedule appears as an 8-period schedule: day 1 includes 4 classes and day 2 includes the remaining 4 classes. Each class meets for 80–90 minutes. Periods 3 and 7 are extended by 30 minutes for lunch. Like other extended-time schedules, professional development is essential to maximize the instructional time. This schedule can be implemented at both the middle and high school levels and may house numerous inserts. While bells ring at fixed times, they may be overridden by inserts. Over the two-day period, the teacher teaches 5 of 8 or 6 of 8 classes. The student attends all 8 classes concurrently.

Table 4.7 Day 1/Day 2 Middle School Teacher Schedule

Day 1		Day 2	
Period	**Course**	**Period**	**Course**
1	English 8–01	5	Intervention
2	H English 8–01	6	English 8–03
3	Team Meeting/ Personal Plan	7	Team Meeting/ Personal Plan
4	English 8–02	8	English 8–04

Table 4.8 Day 1/Day 2 Middle School Student Schedule

Day 1		Day 2	
Period	**Course**	**Period**	**Course**
1	Physical Education	5	Intervention
2	English	6	Spanish II
3	Social Studies	7	Algebra I
4	Art (Semester 1) Technology (Semester 2)	8	Science

Trimester

Most often, only high schools use a trimester schedule, but middle schools sometimes use it for their exploratory/elective classes to provide longer exposure to those classes. In the trimester schedule, the school year is divided into three equal 12-week periods. Each of those time periods includes five 70–72-minute periods with a teacher being assigned to teach 4 of 5 periods each trimester.

A class that in a traditional schedule would meet for the entire year meets for two trimesters in the trimester schedule. Occasionally, those trimesters may not be consecutive. Some classes may meet for only one trimester; others may meet for three trimesters. The decisions on the number of trimesters a course may meet needs to be carefully monitored or the trimester schedule will become a de facto traditional schedule. Students may earn 7½ credits in one school year rather than 6 credits in a 6-period day or 7 credits in a 7-period day.

Table 4.9 Trimester Teacher Schedule

Trimester 1			Trimester 2			Trimester 3	
1	Algebra I A-01		6	Algebra I A-05		11	Algebra I B-03
2	Algebra I A-02		7	Algebra I A-06		12	Algebra I B-04
3	Plan		8	Plan		13	Plan
4	Algebra I A-03		9	Algebra I B-01		14	Algebra I B-05
5	Algebra I A-04		10	Algebra I B-02		15	Algebra I B-06

Table 4.10 Trimester Student Schedule

Trimester 1			Trimester 2			Trimester 3	
1	English 10 A		6	US History B		11	Chemistry B
2	US History A		7	Art II A		12	Spanish III A
3	Physical Education A		8	English 10 B		13	Art II B
4	Chemistry A		9	Geometry A		14	Geometry B
5	Spanish II A		10	Spanish II B		15	Technology A

In case of staff reduction need, the trimester schedule allows for elective positions to be retained. Further, the student has a greater opportunity for electives than in a traditional 6-period day schedule. As in a semester 1/semester 2 or day 1/day 2 schedule, professional development for teaching in extended-time periods becomes essential to the success of the trimester schedule.

Inserts

Inserts exist as subsets or independent variables within any of the primary frameworks to create the master schedule. Their application provides flexibility in which teachers are able to control time. Appearing in K–5, K–6, K–8, middle, or high school schedules, inserts may have a major impact on student achievement as well as graduation rates. If a school is restructuring, inserts can be phased in over time.

Double English/Double Math

Double periods in English and math appear in elementary and middle schools as well as freshman academies. In this insert, English and math periods exist as 80–90 minutes daily. These time periods offer opportunities to enhance student achievement, address Tier 1 interventions, and integrate all aspects of the English/language arts (ELA) curriculum.

Double English/double math inserts fit within the traditional, semester 1/semester 2, and day 1/day 2 primary options. It can further function as a two-teacher team in K–5, K–6, K–8, or grades 6, 7, 8 configuration.

Table 4.11 Double English/Double Math Elementary Teacher Schedule

Mods	1 and 2	3	4	5	6 and 7	8	9
Teacher	ELA	SS	Plan	Lunch	Math	Science	Intervention

Table 4.12 Double English/
Double Math Middle
School Teacher Schedule

Period	Subject
1	Math 01
2	
3	Intervention
4	Lunch
5	Math 02
6	
7	Math 03
8	
9	Team Meeting
10	Plan

Table 4.13 Double English/Double
Math Middle School Student Schedule

Period	Subject
1	Math 01
2	
3	Intervention
4	Lunch
5	ELA
6	
7	Social Studies
8	Science
9	Physical Education/Band
10	Art/Technology/Consumer Science/Music

Table 4.14 Double English/Double Math Freshman Academy

Teacher	1	2	3	4	5	6	7	8	9	10
ELA 1	01	01	Team Meeting	02	02	Lunch	03	03	Plan	Intervention
ELA 2	04	04	Team Meeting	05	05	Lunch	06	06	Plan	Intervention
Social Studies	03	06	Team Meeting	01	04	Lunch	02	05	Plan	Intervention
Science	06	03	Team Meeting	04	01	Lunch	05	02	Plan	Intervention
Math 1	02	02	Team Meeting	03	03	Lunch	01	01	Plan	Intervention
Math 2	05	05	Team Meeting	06	06	Lunch	04	04	Plan	Intervention
Special Education			Team Meeting			Lunch			Plan	Intervention

Credit Recovery

The credit recovery insert applies only to high school schedules. With this insert, the student actually repeats a failed course rather than being assigned a software package to make up the credit. By assigning the student to a teacher-taught course, the student receives the same curriculum possibly from the same teacher and is more likely to remain on track for graduation.

Table 4.15 Credit Recovery High School
Student Schedule

Period	Course
1	English 10/11
2	
3	American History
4	Chemistry
5	Lunch
6	Physical Education
7	Chorus
8	Geometry/Algebra II
9	

Rotational

The rotational approach meets the request of some high school teachers to teach within a 60-minute period rather than either a 45-minute or a 90-minute period. Consequently, although elementary and middle schools have adopted the concept on a more flexible basis, this approach is primarily used in high schools.

Besides altering the length of the class period, the rotational schedule addresses the student's circadian rhythms by altering the time of day various classes meet. Part-time or shared staff becomes one impediment that may limit the potential of the rotations.

In the examples, the schedule presents a 9-period day. Students experience 6 of 9 periods each day. Teachers see 4 classes per day but see each class two times in a three-day rotation. In Table 4.16, one non-teaching period is placed in each of the three segments of the day. Lunch is a module of time not a full period.

Table 4.16 Rotational High School Teacher Schedule

Period	Actual Schedule	Rotating Day 1 (60 minutes)	Rotating Day 2 (60 minutes)	Rotating Day 3 (60 minutes)
1	Plan	Plan	English 10–01	H English 10–01
2	H English 10–01	H English 10–01	Plan	English 10–01
3	English 10–01			
4	English 10–02	English 10–02	Journalism 01	Duty
5	Duty	Duty	English 10–02	Journalism 01
6	Journalism 01			
7	H English 10–02	H English 10–02	Department Meeting	English 10–03
8	English 10–03	English 10–03	H English 10–02	Department Meeting
9	Department Meeting			

Single-Subject Team

A single-subject team focuses on enhancing or differentiating instruction in a specific course. Two teachers of the same content area and,

Table 4.17 Rotational High School Student Schedule

Period	Actual Schedule	Rotating Day 1 (60 minutes)	Rotating Day 2 (60 minutes)	Rotating Day 3 (60 minutes)
1	H English III	H English III	Art	Pre-Calculus
2	Pre-Calculus	Pre-Calculus	H English III	Art
3	Art			
4	H US History	H US History	Spanish III	Choir
5	Choir	Choir	H US History	Spanish III
6	Spanish III			
7	Physical Education	Physical Education	Probability & Statistics	Chemistry
8	Chemistry	Chemistry	Physical Education	Probability & Statistics
9	Probability & Statistics			

if desired, a special education co-teacher, are scheduled for the same 50 students in the same period(s) of the day. On a fluid basis, teachers group and regroup students for enrichment as well as remediation. Available data and ongoing formative assessments determine those decisions. The arrangement encourages students as well as teachers to perceive themselves as a unified team of 50 students with two teachers or three if a co-teacher is involved. Neither teacher should be the permanent enrichment or remediation teacher. Grades are determined by an agreed upon unified grading process so that grades do not become an issue. Single-subject teaming can be applied to any course.

Interdisciplinary-Maximum Flexibility

Interdisciplinary-maximum flexibility provides an opportunity for a cohort of teachers to share the same students for the same periods

Table 4.18 Single-Subject High School Team

Teacher	1	2	3	4	5	6	7	8
Teacher 1	Algebra II-01	Plan	Algebra II-03	Lunch	Geom-etry 01	Plan	Geo n-etry 02	Geom-etry 03
Teacher 2	Algebra II-02	Plan	Algebra II-04	Lunch	Pre-Calcu-lus 01	Pre-Calcu-lus 02	Plan	Pre-Calcu-lus 03
Special Educa-tion	Co-taught	Plan	Co-taught	Lunch				

of the day, enabling flexibility as well as the opportunity for teache
to manage time. A typical cohort includes an English, social studies,
mathematics, and science teacher who share the same 100 students for
the same periods of the day.

This cohort of teachers has common planning time in which
they focus on addressing student needs as determined by data,
observation, and reports from school student personnel staff such
as school psychologists, social workers, and counselors. Designated
times or days determine agendas for development of curriculum,
common testing, teaching practices, curriculum integration, personalization strategies, and creative uses of time. In this period, teachers determine forms of flexibility needed to achieve their team and
instructional goals. Flexibility formats include altering the sequence
of classes, large group instruction, extended-time experiences,
grouping and regrouping of students, time for interdisciplinary experiences, project time, and implementing a flex/advisory/intervention
program.

An interdisciplinary-maximum flexibility schedule fits elementary,
K–8, middle, and high school schedules. Not only can students be
individually scheduled, but the format facilitates transitions from elementary to middle and middle to high school. At the high school level,
the interdisciplinary-maximum flexibility schedule facilitates freshman

academies, magnets, houses, or career pathways as a method to address student needs and focus on student achievement.

Table 4.19 Interdisciplinary-Maximum Flexibility Middle
School Teacher Schedule

Subject	1	2	3	4	5	6	7	8
English	H-01	01 CT	02	03 CT	Lunch	Team Meeting	Inter-vention	Plan
Social Studies	01	02	03	04	Lunch	Team Meeting	Inter-vention	Plan
Math	8–01	Alge-bra I–01	8–02 CT	Alge-bra I–02	Lunch	Team Meeting	Inter-vention	Plan
Science	01	02	03	04	Lunch	Team Meeting	Inter-vention	Plan
Special Ed	Replace-ment English	Co-taught English	Co taught Math	Co-taught English	Lunch	Team Meeting	Inter-vention	Plan

Table 4.20 Interdisciplinary-Maximum Flexibility
Freshman Academy Student Schedule

Period	Course
1	H English
2	Geometry
3	Global Studies
4	Lunch
5	Biology
6	Biology Lab/Physical Education
7	Mandarin II
8	Band

Interdisciplinary-Limited Flexibility

In the interdisciplinary-limited flexibility schedule, all opportunities for flexibility do not exist. In many cases, this schedule occurs because the number of teaching sections exceeds the number of teachers on a team. Consequently, one or two sections must leave the team (sections away) for an elective or another required course. High school magnets, houses, and academies often use this schedule. Like the interdisciplinary-maximum flexibility schedule with a common planning time for team and data meetings, this schedule provides opportunities to integrate the curriculum, respond to student needs and data, and discuss appropriate teaching strategies. Teachers can meet on an interdisciplinary as well as single-subject basis.

Table 4.21 Interdisciplinary-Limited Flexibility Day 1/Day 2
Health Careers Magnet Schedule

	Day 1				Day 2			
Course	**1**	**2**	**3**	**4**	**5**	**6**	**7**	**8**
English	01	02	TM/P	03	04	05	TM/I	06
Social Studies	01	02	TM/P	03	04	05	TM/F	06
Math	Alg. I-01	Alg. II-01	TM/P	Alg. II-02	Geo. 01	H Geo. 01	TM/P	Geo. 2
Chemistry	01	02	TM/P	03	04	05	TM/P	0
Nursing		01	TM/P		02			
Pre-Med	01	02	TM/P			03		
Office Management			TM/P	01	02			03
Physical Therapy	01		TM/P			02		03
Sections Away	**0**	**0**	**6**	**1**	**0**	**0**	**6**	**0**

Interdisciplinary Exploratory/Elective

At the middle school level, teachers of art, music, physical education, technology, and family/consumer science meet in common planning

Table 4.22 Interdisciplinary-Limited Flexibility Day 1/Day 2
Middle School With Team Meeting and Department Meeting

	Day 1				Day 2			
Course	**1**	**2**	**3**	**4**	**5**	**6**	**7**	**8**
English	TM/P	01 CT	02 CT	03	DM/P	04	05	06
Social Studies	TM/P	01	02	03	04	DM/P	05	06
Math	TM/P	01	02	03	04 CT	05 CT	DM/P	06
Science	TM/P	01	02	03	04	05	06	DM/P
Special Education	TM/P	Co-Taught English	Co-Taught English		Co-Taught Math	Co-Taught Math		
Sections Away	**6**	**2**	**2**	**2**	**3**	**3**	**3**	**3**

Table 4.23 Interdisciplinary Exploratory/Elective
Ninth Grade Student Schedule

Period	**Course**
1	English 9
2	Biology
3	Biology Lab/Physical Education
4	Lunch
5	Geometry
6	US History
7	French I
8	Health Careers (Quarter 1)
	Communications Careers (Quarter 2)
	Visual and Performing Arts Careers (Quarter 3)
	Business and Marketing Careers (Quarter 4)

time. During this time, teachers can develop interdisciplinary units and flex time as possible. In high school, CTE teachers meet to discuss their curriculum and to provide students with the opportunity to explore CTE offerings and career pathways that are available in the curriculum.

Table 4.24 Interdisciplinary Exploratory/Elective Middl
School Teachers Schedule

Subject	1	2	3	4	5	6	7	8	9
Physical Education 1	6	6	Team Meeting	Lunch	7	7	Plan	8	8
Physical Education 2	6	6	Team Meeting	Lunch	7	7	Plan	8	8
Art	6	6	Team Meeting	Lunch	7	7	Plan	8	8
STEM	6	6	Team Meeting	Lunch	7	7	Plan	8	8
Guitar	6	6	Team Meeting	Lunch	7	7	Plan	8	
Family/ Consumer Science	6	6	Team Meeting	Lunch	7	7	Plan	8	8
Band	6	6	Team Meeting	Lunch	7	7	Plan	8	8
Choir	6	6	Team Meeting	Lunch	7	7	Plan	8	8

Combination Teams

In a version of interdisciplinary teaming, combination teams focus on curriculum integration and flexible use of time. Generally, English pairs with social studies and math with science. In the middle school, this

Table 4.25 Combination Team Teacher Schedule

Teacher	1	2	3	4	5	6	7	8
English	10–01	10–02	Team Plan	Lunch	10–03	10–04	H 10–01	Plan
US History	10–02	10–01	Team Plan	Lunch	10–04	10–03	Plan	H 10–01
Special Education	Co-taught		Team Plan	Lunch				

Table 4.26 Combination Team Student Schedule

Period	Course
1	English 10/US History
2	
3	Chorus
4	French III
5	Lunch
6	Geometry/Physics
7	
8	Physical Education

Table 4.27 Frameworks and Their Grade Level Application

	K–5 or 6	K–8	6–7–8	9–12
Primary				
Traditional	√	√	√	√
Semester 1/ Semester 2				√
Day 1/Day 2		√	√	√
Trimester		Exploratory/ Elective only	Exploratory/ Elective only	√
Inserts				
Double English/ Double Math	√	√	√	Freshman Academy Only
Credit Recovery				√
Rotational			√	√
Single-Subject	√	√	√	√
Interdisciplinary- Maximum Flexibility	√	√	√	√
Interdisciplinary- Limited Flexibility		√	√	√
Interdisciplinary Exploratory/ Elective	√	√	√	√
Combination			√	√

model could replace a full interdisciplinary team. Again, for successful implementation of this model, common planning time is essential.

Recap

Knowledge of structural frameworks aids in the development of an efficient and equitable master schedule. Blending primary options with one or more inserts provides opportunities to address the needs of various groups of students and enhance college and career readiness. The selection of primary options and inserts is a joint responsibility of all stakeholders. Chapters 5–8 contain a step-by-step approach to building schedules for K–5 or 6, K–8, middle, and high schools. Examples and tables illustrate the steps.

Points to Consider

1. How do the primary frameworks fit the culture of our school or district?

2. What are the pros and cons of each primary framework?

3. How can each insert address the strengths and needs of our students?

4. How can all stakeholders be involved in the process of selecting primary frameworks and inserts?

Steps in Building a K–5 or K–6 Schedule

Focus

- Fourteen steps to build a K–5 or K–6 schedule
- Tables and examples to illustrate steps

Focusing on an elementary type schedule, this chapter walks the scheduling committee through 14 steps to achieve the schedule that best fits the school and its students. For each step, examples illustrate how each step is applied.

Step 1: Review, Revise, or Create a Mission/Vision Statement

As in the classroom where target learning guides the instruction, the mission/vision statement serves as the target for decision-making. This is no less true in seeking out an efficient and equitable schedule than in seeking the curriculum that best meets the needs of the students to be served. It influences the desired outcomes of specific features applied to the schedule as well as all facets within the school day.

Step 2: Gain Faculty Understanding and Support

Any decision that affects faculty and must be implemented by them benefits from their expertise. During scheduling discussions, aspects of scheduling require understanding such as its purpose and the operation of collaboration, intervention, and flexibility. After the schedule has been designed and approved, the knowledge base of the faculty prepares them to explain the schedule to students, parents board of education members, and the community. In the teachers' preparation, the principal informs and encourages them to use the schedule in their daily decision-making.

Step 3: Prepare for the Three Tiers of RtI

Response to Intervention (RtI) philosophies and practice in the district need to be in place and understood by all stakeholders. While Tier 1 interventions are best accomplished by providing opportunities for learning by implementing extended-time periods in the core classroom, Tiers 2 and 3 are best met when the schedule offers an intervention/enrichment period. To meet their students' specific RtI needs, grade level teachers should explore scheduling design for the implementation of that intervention/enrichment period.

During common planning time, teachers make decisions about placement and levels of RtI relying on student data and feedback from all teachers and support staff. In part, their decisions need to assure the fluidity of movement for students within the Tier 2 and 3 designations. Additionally, the specials portion of the schedule should provide these students with opportunities for exploratory experiences as well as intense interventions.

Step 4: Create Modular Grid for Teaching Sections

Based on projected enrollment and staffing allocation, create a grid that lists the number of sections per grade level in the grade and sections columns. Include co-taught students in the sections where they will be housed. Later in this process, special education, ELL, and specials teachers will be listed. Relying on the teachers' contract and number of periods needed to provide the specials program, approximate the number of minutes in an instructional module. In Table 5.1, 40–45 minutes comprise each of the nine instructional modules.

Step 5: Confirm FTE, Sections, Common Plan Periods

At this point, confirmation of the total number of classroom FTE takes place. The decision is based on grade level projected enrollment, number of grade level sections desired, and the number of common planning periods needed. Ideally, all core classroom teachers of a grade level will have a common plan period that occurs when students are in specials.

Step 6: Confirm the Curriculum Chart

Create or review the curriculum chart (K–5 or K–6) including the specials offered and the frequency of special courses. These entries organize the school day and provide the mechanism for delivering the curriculum. Since the contractual length of the school day determines the number of minutes per course or period, each district personalizes this aspect of its schedule. Table 5.2 illustrates a guide for K–6 core subjects.

Table 5.1 Elementary Modular Grid

Grade	Section	01	02	03	04	05	06	07	08	09
P-K	01									
	02									
	03									
	04									
K	01									
	02									
	03									
	04									
1	01									
	02									
	03									
	04									
2	01									
	02									
	03									
	04									

Grade	Section	01	02	03	04	05	06	07	08	09
3	01									
	02									
	03									
	04									
4	01									
	02									
	03									
	04									
5	01									
	02									
	03									
	04									
6	01									
	02									
	03									

Table 5.2 Elementary Grid for Course Minutes per Day

Curriculum Chart							
Curriculum Area	**K**	**1**	**2**	**3**	**4**	**5**	**6**
Reading/Language Arts	120	110	100	90	85	85	83
Mathematics	70	70	80	90	85	85	83
Social Studies	30	35	35	35	40	40	42
Science	30	35	35	35	40	40	42
Total Minutes	**250**	**250**	**250**	**250**	**250**	**250**	**250**

Several factors influence the curriculum of the specials portion of the day:

● the experiences intended to be provided for K–5 or K–6 students;

● desired frequency of class meetings;

● capacity of core classroom sections to attend specials at the same time to enable common planning time for a cohort of teachers.

As a key factor in determining the FTE needed for the school, the specials portion of the curriculum needs careful planning. Tables 5.3 and 5.4 present examples of a specials portion of the schedule and the frequency of those class meetings.

Table 5.3 Scheduling for Frequency of
Four Specials Classes

Frequency of Four Specials Classes	
Special	**Frequency**
Physical Education	3/6 days
Art	1/6 days
Music	1/6 days
Computers	1/6 days
Minutes per Day	**40**

Table 5.4 Scheduling for Frequency of Three Specials Classes

Frequency of Three Specials Classes	
Special	**Frequency**
Physical Education	2/4 days
Art	1/4 days
Music	1/4 days
Minutes per Day	**40**

Step 7: Project Number of Specials Teachers

After projecting the number of specials teachers needed to acco nmo-
date specials courses, add this number of FTE to the established rid.
At this point, review the following:

- teachers' contract to determine class size limitations;
- number of inclusion students in a classroom;
- length of lunch period;
- length of daily planning period provided to core and specials teachers.

While the number of specials teachers determines the number of core
teachers who can attend each common planning period, the number
of common planning periods determines the number of modules or
periods in the school day.

Step 8: Place Specials, Lunch, and Intervention on the Grid

Spread the three components to provide consecutive periods for read-
ing/language arts, mathematics, and possibly social studies and science.
In some cases, the intervention period may be the responsibility of the

Table 5.5 Grid to Determine Section and Specials Distribution

Grade	Section	01	02	03	04	05	06	07	08	09
P-K	1									
	2									
	3									
	4									
K	1									
	2									
	3									
	4									
1	1									
	2									
	3									
	4									
2	1									
	2									
	3									
	4									

Grade	Section	01	02	03	04	05	06	07	08	09
3	1									
	2									
	3									
	4									
4	1									
	2									
	3									
	4									
5	1									
	2									
	3									
	4									
6	1									
	2									
	3									
	4									

Grade	Section	01	02	03	04	05	06	07	08	09
Specials	PE 1									
	PE 2									
	Art									
	Music									

grade-level teachers; in others, an intervention team supports the core teachers. The intervention team comprises a variety of specialists: special education and ELL teachers as well as a literacy coach and/or a math coach. Consequently, to facilitate these resources, the intervention periods need to be spread throughout the school day. Table 5.6 accomplishes that spread.

Step 9: Place Core Classes on the Grid

After placing specials, lunch, and intervention periods on the grid, add core classes for each grade. Focus on creating consecutive periods especially for reading/language arts and math. If necessary, adjust the previous entries of specials, lunch, and intervention periods to allow core consecutive periods.

If grades 5 and 6 are addressed as middle school grades, a different schedule is possible. Add a tenth module to accommodate a middle school program of studies. With the module addition, two planning periods allow for a team meeting and a personal planning time. The planning periods affect the length of each instructional module. Additionally, a two-teacher team structure indicated in Table 5.7 enhances subject matter specialization in light of local, state, and national testing programs.

Step 10: Indicate ELL and Special Education Teachers

Following a review of language levels and IEPs for the coming school year, indicate ELL and special education teachers—co-taught, replacement, and pull-out. Table 5.8 reflects periods assigned for intervention. During the open periods, these teachers provide push-in or pull-out services. Simultaneously, consider other diverse populations.

Table 5.6 Specials, Lunch, and Interventions Grid

Grades P-K ½ day, K, 1, 2

Grade	Section	01	02	03	04	05	06	07	08	09
P-K ½ day	01						I			S
	02					L	I			S
	03					L	I			S
	04					L	I			S
K	01			I	L			S	I	
	02			I	L			S	I	
	03			I	L			S	I	
	04			I	L			S	I	
1	01				L			S	S	I
	02				L			S	S	I
	03				L			S	S	I
	04				L			S	S	I
2	01					L	S	I		
	02					L	S	I		
	03					L	S	I		
	04					L	S	I		

Grades 3, 4, 5, 6

Grade	Section	01	02	03	04	05	06	07	08	09
3	01					L	I		I	
	02					L	I		I	S
	03					L	I		I	S
	04					L	I		I	S
4	01			S				S	S	I
	02			S				S	S	I
	03			S				S	S	I
	04			S				S	S	I
5	01	I			S		L	I		
	02	I			S		L	I		
	03	I			S		L	I		
	04	I			S		L	I		
6	01	S				I	L			
	02	S				I	L			
	03	S				I	L			
	04	S				I	L			

Specials

Section	01	02	03	04	05	06	07	08	09
PE 1	6	P	4	5	L	2	K	1	3
PE 2	6	P	4	5	L	2	K	1	3
Art	6	P	4	5	L	2	K	1	3
Music	6	P	4	5	L	2	K	1	3

Table 5.7 Addition of Core Subjects to Grid

Grade	Section	01	02	03	04	05	06	07	08	09
P-K ½ day	01									
	02									
	03									
	04									
K	01	R/LA		I	L	Math		S	SS	Sci
	02	R/LA		I	L	Math		S	SS	Sci
	03	R/LA		I	L	Math		S	SS	Sci
	04	R/LA		I	L	Math		S	SS	Sci
1	01	R/LA		SS	L	Sci	Math	S	S	I
	02	R/LA		SS	L	Sci	Math	S	S	I
	03	R/LA		SS	L	Sci	Math	S	S	I
	04	R/LA		SS	L	Sci	Math	S	S	I
2	01	R/LA		Math		L	S	I	SS	Sci
	02	R/LA		Math		L	S	I	SS	Sci
	03	R/LA		Math		L	S	I	SS	Sci
	04	R/LA		Math		L	S	I	SS	Sci
3	01	R/LA		Math		L	I	SS	Sci	S
	02	R/LA		Math		L	I	SS	Sci	S
	03	R/LA		Math		L	I	SS	Sci	S
	04	R/LA		Math		L	I	SS	Sci	S
4	01	R/LA		S	SS	L	Math	I	Sci	
	02	R/LA		S	SS	L	Math	I	Sci	
	03	R/LA		S	SS	L	Math	I	Sci	
	04	R/LA		S	SS	L	Math	I	Sci	

Continued

Table 5.7 Continued

Grade	Section	01	02	03	04	05	06	07	08	09
5 A	R/LA/SS	I	01		S	01	L	02		
	Math/Sci	I	02		S	02	L	01		
5 B	R/LA/SS	I	03		S	03	L	04		
	Math/Sci	I	04		S	04	L	03		

Grade	Section	01	02	03	04	05	06	07	08	09
6 A	R/LA/SS	S	01			I	L	02		
	Math/Sci	S	02			I	L	01		
6 B	R/LA/SS	S	03			I	L	04		
	Math/Sci	S	04			I	L	03		

	Section	01	02	03	04	05	06	07	08	09
Specials	PE 1	6	P	4	5	L	2	K	1	3
	PE 2	6	P	4	5	L	2	K	1	3
	Art	6	P	4	5	L	2	K	1	3
	Music	6	P	4	5	L	2	K	1	3

Table 5.8 ELL and Special Education Teachers Support Intervention Period

Grade	Section	01	02	03	04	05	06	07	08	09
P-K ½ day	01									
K	01	R/LA		I	L	Math		S	SS	Sci
	02	R/LA		I	L	Math		S	SS	Sci
	03	R/LA		I	L	Math		S	SS	Sci
	04	R/LA		I	L	Math		S	SS	Sci
1	01	R/LA		SS	L	Sci	Math	S	I	
	02	R/LA		SS	L	Sci	Math	S	I	
	03	R/LA		SS	L	Sci	Math	S	I	
	04	R/LA		SS	L	Sci	Math	S	I	
2	01	R/LA		Math		L	S	I	SS	Sci
	02	R/LA		Math		L	S	I	SS	Sci
	03	R/LA		Math		L	S	I	SS	Sci
	04	R/LA		Math		L	S	I	SS	Sci
3	01	R/LA		Math		L	I	SS	Sci	S
	02	R/LA		Math		L	I	SS	Sci	S
	03	R/LA		Math		L	I	SS	Sci	S
	04	R/LA		Math		L	I	SS	Sci	S
4	01	R/LA		S	SS	L	Math	I		Sci
	02	R/LA		S	SS	L	Math	I		Sci
	03	R/LA		S	SS	L	Math	I		Sci
	04	R/LA		S	SS	L	Math	I		Sci

Continued

Table 5.8 Continued

Grade	Section	01	02	03	04	05	06	07	08	09
5 A	R/LA/SS	I	01		S	01	L	02		
	Math/Sci	I	02		S	02	L	01		
5 B	R/LA/SS	I	03		S	03	L	04		
	Math/Sci	I	04		S	04	L	03		

Grade	Section	01	02	03	04	05	06	07	08	09
6 A	R/LA/SS	S	01			I	L	02		
	Math/Sci	S	02			I	L	01		
6 B	R/LA/SS	S	03			I	L	04		
	Math/Sci	S	04			I	L	03		

Section	01	02	03	04	05	06	07	08	09
ELL 1		P	K	L		3	2		1
Sp. Ed 1		P	K	L		3	2		1
Sp. Ed 2		P	K	L		3	2		1
ELL 2	5	P		L	6			4	
Sp. Ed 3	5	P		L	6			4	
Sp. Ed 4	5	P		L	6			4	
Specials PE 1	6	P	4	5	L	2	K	1	3
PE 2	6	P	4	5	L	2	K	1	3
Art	6	P	4	5	L	2	K	1	3
Music	6	P	4	5	L	2	K	1	3

Step 11: Provide Common Planning Time for Specials Teachers and Intervention Team

Opportunities for common planning time for intervenion team teachers aid the integration and consistency of curriculum and instruction. Some intervention team members are already included in the FTE count, e.g., special education and ELL teachers. In common planning time, specials teachers become aware of curriculum units in the core classrooms for content integration and enrichment experiences.

Table 5.9 Specials Teachers' Schedule

	1	2	3	4	5	6	7	8	9
PE 1	6	P	4	5	L	2	K	1	3
PE 2	6	P	4	5	L	2	K	1	3
Art	6	P	4	5	L	2	K	1	3
Music	6	P	4	5	L	2	K	1	3

Table 5.10 Intervention Team Schedule

	1	2	3	4	5	6	7	8	9
Sp. Ed 1		P	K	L		3	2		
Sp. Ed 2		P	K	L		3	2		
Sp. Ed 3	5	P		L	6			4	
Sp. Ed 4	5	P		L	6			4	
ELL 1		P	K	L		3	2		1
ELL 2	5	P		L	6			4	
Math Support	5	P	K	L		3	2	4	1
Literacy Support	5	P	K	L	6		2	4	1

Step 12: Establish Rotation for Specials

Table 5.11 Specials Rotation Schedule

Section	Day 1	Day 2	Day 3	Day 4
01	PE 1	Art	PE 1	Music
02	Music	PE 1	Art	PE 1
03	PE 2	Music	PE 2	Art
04	Art	PE 2	Music	PE 2

Step 13: Finalize FTE

Based on projected enrollment, sections to be created, and staffing needs for specials and intervention programs, finalize the number of FTEs for each school.

Step 14: Professional Development

To best support the chosen schedule, plan significant professional development that focuses on teacher and support staff collaboration, use of data, flexibility, and effective use of extended-time modules. Throughout the year, follow-up training and schedule implementation discussions aid the consistency desired.

Recap

Opportunities for collaboration, interventions, and flexibility guide the development of a K–5 or K–6 schedule. At the district level, the super-intendent and other central office personnel support the efforts of each individual school to assure consistency. Building principals monitor the efficient and equitable distribution of FTEs to meet the needs of all students. Stakeholders conduct a systematic assessment of the steps outlined in this chapter on a continuous basis. Many school districts choose to modify the K–5 or K–6 model to K–8, the topic of the next chapter.

Points to Consider

1. How has the mission/vision statement guided our work in building the schedule?

2. In developing the schedule, how did the committee gain faculty understanding and support?

3. In what ways does the schedule enable teachers to implement the three tiers of RtI?

4. How does the master schedule set the stage for interdisciplinary team structure?

5. How does the master schedule set the stage for possible interdisciplinary team structure and subject matter specialists?

6. What are the goals of common planning time?

7. What opportunities exist for specials teachers and members of the intervention team to have common planning time?

8. Does the schedule accommodate the district curriculum chart?

9. Does the number of specials teachers allow common planning time for each teacher of a grade level?

10. In what ways does the schedule meet the needs of a diverse population?

11. What opportunities for regrouping or multi-age instruction exist in reading/language arts and math at each grade level?

12. How does the schedule feature the least restrictive environment for all students?

13. How will the professional development program provide for implementation of the master schedule?

14. In what ways does the professional development program encourage teachers to take ownership of the schedule?

15. To what extent are schedules within the district consistent with each other?

6 | Steps in Building a K–8 Schedule

Focus

- Fifteen steps to design a K–8 schedule
- Tables and examples to illustrate steps

This chapter walks the scheduling committee through 15 steps to achieve the schedule that best fits the K–8 school and its students. Within a designated elementary school building, the schedule combines a middle school schedule with an elementary schedule. Examples illustrate the application of many steps.

Step 1: Review, Revise, or Create a Mission/Vision Statement

As in a classroom where target learning guides the instruction, the mission/vision statement serves as the target for decision-making. This is no less true in seeking out an efficient and equitable schedule than in seeking the curriculum that best meets the needs of the students to be served. Specific features of the mission/vision statement influence the desired outcomes to achieve a K–8 experience.

Step 2: Gain Faculty Understanding and Support

Any decision that affects faculty and must be implemented by them benefits from their expertise. In a K–8 building that seeks to combine elementary and middle school schedules, faculty input assumes an important role. During scheduling discussions, aspects of scheduling require understanding by all grade levels involved. Those aspects include the purpose of the schedule and the operation of collaboration, intervention, and flexibility to implement the schedule. The resulting knowledge base of the faculty prepares them to explain the approved schedule to students, parents, board of education members, and the community. In the teachers' preparation, the principal informs and encourages them to use the schedule in their daily decision-making.

Step 3: Prepare for the Three Tiers of RtI

RtI philosophies and practice in the district need to be in place and understood by all stakeholders. While Tier 1 interventions are best accomplished by providing opportunities for learning by implementing extended-time periods for the core classroom, Tiers and 3 are best met when the schedule offers an intervention/enrichment period. To meet their students' specific RtI needs, grade-level teachers should explore scheduling designs for the implementation of that intervention/enrichment period.

During common planning time, teachers make decisions about placement and levels of RtI relying on student data and feedback from all teachers and support staff. In part, their decisions need to assure the fluidity of movement for students within the Tier 2 and 3 designations. Additionally, the specials portion of the schedule should provide these students with opportunities for exploratory experiences as well as intense interventions.

Step 4: Create a Modular Grid for Teaching Sections

Based on projected enrollment and staffing allocation, create a grid that lists the number of sections per grade level in the grade column and the potential number of instructional modules. Because of the elementary segment, the sample grid in Table 6.1 implies the use of a traditional 8–12 module day. Include co-taught students in the sections where they will be housed. Later in this process, special education, ELL, and specials teachers will be listed. Relying on the teachers' contract and number of periods needed to provide the specials program, approximate the length or number of minutes in an instructional module. In the sample grid, each of the 10 instructional modules comprises 40 minutes. Opportunities for extended-time periods are provided within the grade-level schedule.

Table 6.1 K–8 Modular Grid

		1	2	3	4	5	6	7	8	9	10
PK	01										
	02										
K	01										
	02										
1	01										
	02										
2	01										
	02										
3	01										
	02										

Continued

Table 6.1 Continued

		1	2	3	4	5	6	7	8	9	10
4	01										
	02										
5	01										
	02										
6	01										
	02										
7	01										
	02										
8	01										
	02										

Step 5: Confirm Number of Modules Needed for Teaching Sections and Common Planning Periods

At this point, confirm the total number of core classroom FTE. The decision is based on grade-level projected enrollment, number of grade-level sections desired, and the number of common planning periods needed. Ideally, all core classroom teachers will have a common plan period that occurs when students are in specials. In smaller schools with an adequate number of specials teachers, two grade levels can plan concurrently.

Step 6: Create or Review the Curriculum Chart K–4 or K–5

Create or review the curriculum chart (K–4 or K–5) including the specials offered and the frequency of specials courses. These entries organize the school day and provide the curriculum to be delivered. Because entries vary among districts, each district personalizes this chart to organize its school day. Table 6.2 illustrates a guide for K–4 or K–5 core subjects. Separate charts follow for specials or exploratory/elective courses.

Table 6.2 K–4 or K–5 Core Course Minutes per Day

Curriculum Chart						
Curriculum Area	K	1	2	3	4	5
Reading/ Language Arts	120	110	100	90	85	85
Mathematics	70	70	80	90	85	85
Social Studies	30	35	35	35	40	40
Science	30	35	35	35	40	40
Total Minutes	250	250	250	250	250	250

Several factors influence the curriculum of the specials portion of the day:

- the experiences intended to be provided for K–4 or K–5 students;
- desired frequency of class meetings;
- capacity of core classroom sections to attend specials at the same time to enable common planning time for a cohort of teachers.

As a key factor in determining the FTE needed for the school, the specials portion of the curriculum needs careful planning. Tables 6.3 and 6.4 present examples of a specials portion of the schedule and the frequency of those class meetings.

Table 6.3 Scheduling for Frequency of Four
Specials Classes

Frequency of Four Specials Classes	
Special	Frequency
Physical Education	3/6 days
Art	1/6 days
Music	1/6 days
Computers	1/6 days
Minutes per Day	40

Table 6.4 Scheduling for Frequency of
Three Specials Classes

Frequency of Three Specials Classes	
Special	**Frequency**
Physical Education	2/4 days
Art	1/4 days
Music	1/4 days
Minutes per Day	**40**

Step 7: Establish Program of Studies for Grades 5–8 or 6–8

Equivalent to the curriculum chart for primary grades, a program of studies chart helps guide the middle grades schedule. This chart is divided into two parts—core and exploratory/elective. Typically, the core section includes reading/language arts, mathematics, science, and social studies. In a K–8 setting and depending on state and district guidelines, the exploratory/elective section may include any of the following: physical education, art, music, technology, family and consumer science, and world languages.

To set the stage for flexibility, the number of periods per day or per week in the core block should not exceed the number of periods per day or per week that teachers are contractually permitted to teach. Because certain options may be appropriate at some grade levels and not others, central office personnel as well as school-based educational leaders should consider the options in Tables 6.5 and 6.6.

Table 6.5 Program of Studies for Grades 5–8 or 6–8 Core Classes

Option	Course(s)	Periods per Week	Grade 5	Grade 6	Grade 7	Grade 8
1	ELA/SS	15				
	Math/Sci	15				
	Total	**30**				

Continued

Option	Course(s)	Periods per Week	Grade 5	Grade 6	Grade 7	Grade 8
2	ELA/SS	12.5				
	Math/Sci	12.5				
	Total	**25**				
3	ELA	7.5				
	SS	7.5				
	Math	7.5				
	Science	7.5				
	Total	**30**				
4	ELA	10				
	SS	5				
	Math	5				
	Science	5				
	Total	**25**				
5	ELA	10				
	SS	5				
	Math	10				
	Science	5				
	Total	**30**				
6	ELA	5				
	SS	5				
	Math	5				
	Science	5				
	World Languages	5				
	Total	**25**				
7	ELA	5				
	SS	5				
	Math	5				
	Science	5				
	Technology	5				
	Total	**25**				

Required as well as elective experiences can be part of the exploratory/elective schedule. The FTE allocation, however, may determine the number of exploratory/elective experiences to be offered. In some schools, Tier 3 intervention, special education support, and ELL supplements comprise a part of the exploratory/elective program. If these options exist, those responsible to create these offerings need to keep in mind the least restrictive environment for all students.

Table 6.6 Program of Studies for Grades 5–8 or 6–8
Exploratory/Elective Classes

Option	Course(s)	Periods per Week	Grade 5	Grade 6	Grade 7	Grade 8
1	PE	5				
	Art/Music	5				
	Total	**10**				
2	PE	2.5				
	Band/Chorus/Gen. Music	2.5				
	Art	2.5				
	Computers	2.5				
	Total	**10**				
3	PE	2.5				
	Select 3 courses @ 2.5 each: Band/ Chorus/Gen. Music/ Computers/Art Tier 3 Math/ Tier 3 Rdg./ ELL Support/Sp. Ed Support	7.5				
	Total	**10**				
4	PE	5				
	Select 2 courses @ 2.5 each: Band/ Chorus/Gen. Music/ Computers/Art Tier 3 Math/ Tier 3 Rdg./ ELL Support/Sp. Ed Support	5				
	Total	**10**				

Step 8: Project Number of Specials Teachers

After projecting the number of specials teachers needed to accommodate the chosen specials courses, add this number of FTE to the established grid. At this point, some cautions are needed:

- review teachers' contract to determine class size limitations;
- length of lunch period;
- length and number of daily planning period(s) provided to core, specials, and exploratory/elective teachers.

The number of specials teachers determines the number of core teachers who can attend each common planning period; therefore, the number of common planning periods determines the number of modules or periods in the school day. While primary (K–4 or K–5) teachers usually have one non-contact period per day, middle grades (5–8, 6–8, and 7–8) teachers benefit from two non-contact periods per day, one being dedicated to common planning time.

Table 6.7 K–8 Modular Grid Adding Specials or Exploratory/Electives Teachers

		1	2	3	4	5	6	7	8	9	10
PK	01										
	02										
K	01										
	02										
1	01										
	02										
2	01										
	02										

Continued

69

Table 6.7 Continued

		1	2	3	4	5	6	7	8	9	10
3	01										
	02										
4	01										
	02										
5	01										
	02										
6	01										
	02										
7	01										
	02										
8	01										
	02										
Specials or Exploratory/ Elective	PE 1										
	PE 2										
	Art										
	Music										
	Tech										
	TBD										

Step 9: Place Specials or Exploratory/ Elective Courses, Lunch, and Intervention Periods on Grid

In order to provide consecutive periods for reading/language arts, mathematics, and possibly science and social studies, spread the three components. The intervention period occurs according to how it is delivered: responsibility of the grade-level teachers or intervention team to support core teachers. Since the intervention team can include a variety of specialists such as special education, ELL, a literary coach, and a math coach, the spreading of these periods throughout the day ensures their ability to serve student needs.

Table 6.8 Placement of Specials, Exploratory/Electives, Lunch, and Intervention Periods on Grid

		1	2	3	4	5	6	7	8	9	10
PK	01				L			S			I
	02				L			S			I
K	01				L			S			I
	02				L			S			I
1	01				L				S	I	
	02				L				S	I	
2	01					L			S	I	
	02					L			S	I	
3	01					L			I	S	
	02					L			I	S	
4	01					L			I	S	
	02					L			I	S	
5	01				S	I	L				S
	02				S	I	L				S
6	01				S	I	L				S
	02				S	I	L				S

Continued

Table 6.8 Continued

		1	2	3	4	5	6	7	8	9	10
7	01	S	S				L	I			
	02	S	S				L	I			
8	01	S	S				L	I			
	02	S	S				L	I			
Specials or Exploratory/ Elective	PE 1	7, 8	7, 8	TM	5, 6	L	P	Pk K	1,2	3, 4	5, 6
	PE 2	7, 8	7, 8	TM	5, 6	L	P	PK, K	1,2	3, 4	5, 6
	Art	7, 8	7, 8	TM	5, 6	L	P	PK, K	1,2	3, 4	5, 6
	Music	7, 8	7, 8	TM	5, 6	L	P	Pk, K	1,2	3, 4	5, 6

Step 10: Place Reading/Language Arts, Mathematics, Science, and Social Studies on the Grid

Following the curriculum chart for primary grades and program of studies for grades 5–8, place reading/language arts, mathematics, science, and social studies on the grid. A focus on providing consecutive periods for core subjects influences the placement of courses and, ultimately, the instructional opportunities for extended time. If necessary, specials or exploratory/elective courses, lunch, and intervention periods may need to be adjusted in order to enhance consecutive core period opportunities. Where appropriate, determine the teaming structure to meet specialization arising due to local, state, and national testing.

In Table 6.9 grades 5 and 6 demonstrate a two-teacher team alignment: one a teacher of English and social studies, the other a teacher of science and math. Grades 7 and 8 exist as a four-teacher team, one teacher for each core subject. Each class meets for 1½ periods per day.

Table 6.9 Placement of Core Subjects on Grid

		1	2	3	4	5	6	7	8	9	10
PK	01	R/LA			L	Math		S	SS	Sci	I
	02	R/LA			L	Math		S	SS	Sci	I
K	01	R/LA			L	Math		S	SS	Sci	I
	02	R/LA			L	Math		S	SS	Sci	I
1	01	R/LA			L	Math		SS	S	I	Sci
	02	R/LA			L	Math		SS	S	I	Sci
2	01	R/LA			Sci	L	Math		S	I	SS
	02	R/LA			Sci	L	Math		S	I	SS
3	01	R/LA			Sci	L	Math		I	S	SS
	02	R/LA			Sci	L	Math		I	S	SS
4	01	R/LA			Sci	L	Math		I	S	SS
	02	R/LA			Sci	L	Math		I	S	SS
5	R/LA/SS	01			S	I	L	02			S
	Math/Sci	02			S	I	L	01			S
6	R/LA/SS	01			S	I	L	02			S
	Math/Sci	02			S	I	L	01			S
7	R/LA	S	S	7–01		7–02		L	I	8–01	8–02
	SS	S	S	7–02		7–01		L	I	8–02	8–01
8	Math	S	S	8–01		8–02		L	I	7–01	7–02
	Science	S	S	8–02		8–01		L	I	7–02	7–01

Continued

Table 6.9 Continued

		1	2	3	4	5	6	7	8	9	10
Specials or Exploratory/ Elective	PE 1	7, 8	7, 8	TM	5, 6	L	P	PK K	1,2	3, 4	5, 6
	PE 2	7, 8	7, 8	TM	5, 6	L	P	PK, K	1,2	3, 4	5, 6
	Art	7, 8	7, 8	TM	5, 6	L	P	PK, K	1,2	3, 4	5, 6
	Music	7, 8	7, 8	TM	5, 6	L	P	PK, K	1,2	3, 4	5, 6

Step 11: Indicate ELL and Special Education Placement on Grid

Using a review of language levels and IEPs for the coming school year, indicate ELL and special education teachers—co-taught, replacement, or pull-out. Other diverse populations may need to be considered as well. These additions to the grid are viewed as placeholders subject to student needs and FTE available.

Table 6.10 Placing ELL and Special Education Teachers

		1	2	3	4	5	6	7	8	9	10
PK	01	R/LA			L	Math		S	S	Sci	I
	02	R/LA			L	Math		S	S	Sci.	I
K	01	R/LA			L	Math		S	SS	Sci.	I
	02	R/LA			L	Math		S	SS	Sci.	I
1	01	R/LA			L	Math		SS	S	I	Sci.
	02	R/LA			L	Math		SS	S	I	Sci.

Continued

		1	2	3	4	5	6	7	8	9	10
2	01	R/LA			Sci	L	Math		S	I	SS
	02	R/LA			Sci	L	Math		S	I	SS
3	01	R/LA			Sci.	L	Math		I	S	SS
	02	R/LA			Sci.	L	Math		I	S	SS
4	01	R/LA			Sci.	L	Math		I	S	SS
	02	R/LA			Sci.	L	Math		I	S	SS
ELL 1											
Sp. Ed 1											
Sp. Ed 2											
5	R/LA/SS	01			S	I	L	02			S
	Math/Sci.	02			S	I	L	01			S
6	R/LA/SS	01			S	I	L	02			S
	Math/Sci.	02			S	I	L	01			S
Sp. Ed 3											
7	R/LA	S	S	7–01		7–02	L	I	8–01		8–02
	SS	S	S	7–02		7–01	L	I	8–02		8–01
8	Math	S	S	8–01		8–02	L	I	7–01		7–02
	Science	S	S	8–02		8–01	L	I	7–02		7–01
ELL 2											
Sp. Ed 4											

Continued

Table 6.10 Continued

		1	2	3	4	5	6	7	8	9	10
Specials or Exploratory/ Elective	PE 1	7, 8	7, 8	TM	5, 6	L	P	PK, K	1,2	3, 4	5, 6
	PE 2	7, 8	7, 8	TM	5, 6	L	P	PK, K	1,2	3, 4	5, 6
	Art	7, 8	7, 8	TM	5, 6	L	P	PK, K	1 2	3, 4	5, 6
	Music	7, 8	7, 8	TM	5, 6	L	P	PK, K	1,2	3, 4	5, 6

Step 12: Provide Common Planning Time Opportunities for Specials, Exploratory/Elective and Intervention Team

Specials teachers as well as exploratory/elective and intervention teams benefit from common planning time. Some of the intervention team teachers may be included in the earlier FTE count. The math or literacy support positions may not have been previously indicated. In Table 6.12 the non-assigned periods provide time for push-in or pull-out services.

Table 6.11 Specials Teachers and Common Planning Time

	1	2	3	4	5	6	7	8	9	10
PE 1	7, 8	7, 8	TM	5, 6	L	P	PK, K	1, 2	3, 4	5, 6
PE 2	7, 8	7, 8	TM	5, 6	L	P	PK, K	1, 2	3, 4	5, 6
Art	7, 8	7, 8	TM	5, 6	L	P	PK, K	1, 2	3, 4	5, 6
Music	7, 8	7, 8	TM	5, 6	L	P	PK, K	1, 2	3, 4	5, 6

Table 6.12 Intervention Team Common Planning Time

	1	2	3	4	5	6	7	8	9	10
Sp. Ed 1			TM					3, 4	1, 2	PK, K
Sp. Ed 2			TM					3, 4	1, 2	PK, K
Sp. Ed 3			TM		5, 6	L	7, 8			
Sp. Ed 4			TM		5, 6	L	7, 8			
ELL 1			TM					3, 4	1, 2	PK, K
ELL 2			TM		5, 6	L	7, 8			
Math Support			TM		5, 6	L	7, 8	3, 4		1, 2
Literacy Support			TM		5, 6	L	7, 8	3, 4		1, 2

Step 13: Establish Rotations for Specials or Exploratory/Elective Subjects

Table 6.13 Establish Rotations for Primary Grade Specials or Exploratory/Elective Subjects

Primary Grades				
Section	Day 1	Day 2	Day 3	Day 4
1–01	PE 1	Art	PE 1	Music
1–02	Music	PE 1	Art	PE 1
2–01	PE 2	Music	PE 2	Art
2–02	Art	PE 2	Music	PE 2

Table 6.14 Establish Rotations for Middle Grade Specials or Exploratory/Elective Subjects

Middle Grades				
	Period 1		Period 2	
Section	Day 1	Day 2	Day 3	Day 4
7–01	PE 1	PE 1	Art	Music
7–02	PE 2	PE 2	Music	Art
8–01	Art	Music	PE 1	PE 1
8–02	Music	Art	PE 2	PE 2

Step 14: Finalize FTE numbers

Using projected enrollment, sections to be created, interventions, and staffing needs for the specials or exploratory/elective programs, finalize the number of FTE needed for each school.

Step 15: Plan Professional Development

Professional development is essential to efficiently and equitably implement the schedule. The agenda for this experience focuses on collaboration, use of data, flexibility, and effective use of extended-time modules. Throughout the remainder of the year, follow-up monitoring and training encourages assimilation of the schedule.

Recap

For a variety of reasons, many school districts create K–8 configurations. Many of these schools tend to be inner-city schools or have low enrollment. While the integrity of the primary/intermediate grades (K–4 or K–5) remains, a hybrid of a typical middle level program appears in this chapter. The degree of middle level implementation depends on the FTE available, the teachers' contract, and district finances. Chapter 7 introduces a comprehensive model for middle schools (grades 5–8, 6–8, or 7–8).

Points to Consider

1. How has the mission/vision statement guided our work in building the schedule?

2. In developing the schedule, how did the committee gain faculty understanding and support?

3. In what ways does the schedule facilitate an understanding of and support for the benefits of the K–8 model?

4. How does the schedule enable teachers to implement the three tiers of RtI?

5. How does the master schedule set the stage for possible interdisciplinary team structure and subject matter specialists?

6. What is the goal for common planning time?

7. What opportunities exist for common planning time for specials, exploratory/elective teachers, and members of the intervention team?

8. To what extent does the schedule accommodate the district curriculum chart and the middle grades program of studies?

9. Does the number of specials and exploratory/elective teachers allow common planning time for cohorts of teachers at a grade level?

10. How does the schedule allow regrouping of students in specials or exploratory/elective courses?

11. In what ways does the schedule meet the needs of a diverse population?

12. Are opportunities for regrouping or multi-age instruction provided?

13. How does the schedule provide opportunities for ELL and special education teachers to address the needs of diverse populations?

14. How does the schedule provide the least restrictive environment for all students?

15. How will the professional development program provide for implementation of the master schedule?

16. In what ways does the professional development program encourage teachers to take ownership of the schedule?

17. To what extent are schedules within the district consistent with each other?

7 Steps in Building a Middle School Schedule

Focus

- Twelve steps to develop a middle school schedule
- Tables and examples illustrate steps

The following 12 steps take the scheduling committee through the process of forming a middle school schedule. The schedule serves as the foundation for implementing the middle school concept in the context and culture of the community.

Step 1: Review, Revise, or Create a Mission/Vision Statement

As in a classroom where target learning guides instruction, the mission/vision statement serves as the target for decision-making. This is no less true in seeking out an efficient and equitable schedule than in seeking the curriculum that best meets the needs of students to be served. It influences the desired outcomes of specific features applied to the schedule as well as all facets within the school day for the middle school experience.

Step 2: Gain Faculty Understanding and Support

Any decision that affects faculty and must be implemented by them benefits from their expertise. During scheduling discussions, aspects of scheduling require understanding by all involved grade-level and exploratory/elective staff. Those aspects include the purpose of the schedule, as well as the operation of collaboration, intervention, and flexibility to implement the schedule. The resulting knowledge base of the faculty prepares them to explain the approved schedule to students, parents, board of education members, and the community. In the teachers' preparation, the principal informs and encourages them to use the schedule in their daily decision-making.

Step 3: Provide for the Three Tiers of RtI

RtI philosophies and practice in the district need to be in place and understood by all stakeholders. While Tier 1 interventions are best accomplished by providing opportunities for learning by implementing extended-time periods for the core classroom, Tiers 2 and 3 are best met when the schedule offers an intervention/enrichment period often in the form of a flex/advisory/intervention period. To meet students' specific RtI needs, grade-level teachers should explore scheduling designs for the implementation of that intervention/enrichment period.

During common planning time, teachers make decisions about placement and levels of RtI relying on student data and feedback from all teachers and support staff. In part, their decisions need to assure the fluidity of movement for students within the Tier 2 and 3 designations. Additionally, the exploratory/elective portion of the schedule should provide these students with opportunities for exploratory experiences as well as intense interventions.

Step 4: Choose Primary Framework and Appropriate Inserts

When choosing the primary framework and inserts, the committee consistently uses the mission/vision statement to guide decisions. Often, middle schools choose a traditional or day 1/day 2 primary framework. Once the primary framework is chosen, delivering the comprehensive curriculum influences the choice of inserts.

Inserts frequently chosen include double English/double math, single-subject teams, interdisciplinary-maximum or limited flexibility teams, interdisciplinary exploratory/elective teams, or combination teams. Since few inserts are mutually exclusive, multiple inserts can be included within the master schedule. In order to ensure successful implementation, the faculty needs to provide input on decisions. Once decisions are made, successful implementation requires professional development that addresses effective implementation of a comprehensive schedule.

Primary Frameworks

- Traditional 6-, 7-, 8-, or 9-Period Day
- Day 1/Day 2

Inserts

- Double English/Double Math
- Single-Subject Team
- Interdisciplinary-Maximum Flexibility Team
- Interdisciplinary-Limited Flexibility Team
- Interdisciplinary Exploratory/Encore Team
- Combination Team

Step 5: Create Bell and Lunch Schedule

While the teachers' contract may determine the length of the lunch period, the primary framework determines placement of the bell and lunch schedules. In a traditional schedule, lunch can be a full period or a 30/35-minute module.

Table 7.1 Traditional Bell and Lunch Schedule

Full Period	Period	Time
	1	8:00–8:45
	2	8:45–9:30
	3	9:30–10:15
Lunch	4	10:15–11:00
Lunch	5	11:00–11:45
Lunch	6	11:45–12:30
	7	12:30–1:15
	8	1:15–2:00
	9	2:00–2:45

Table 7.2 Modular Lunch Schedule

Period	Mod	Time
1	(1)	8:00–8:45
2	(2)	8:50–9:35
3	(3)	9:40–10:25

A			B			C		
Period	Mod	Time	Period	Mod	Time	Period	Mod	Time
Lunch	(4)	10:25–10:55	4	(4–5)	10:30–11:15	4	(4–5)	10:30–11:15
4	(5–6)	11:00–11:45	Lunch	(6)	11:15–11:45	5	(6–7)	11:20–12:05
5	(7–8)	11:50–12:35	5	(7–8)	11:50–12:35	Lunch	(8)	12:05–12:35
			6	(9)	12:40–1:25			
			7	(10)	1:30–2:15			
			(8)	(11)	2:20–3:05			

Day 1/Day 2 schedules require a variation of a modular model in which lunch is embedded in Period 3 of Day 1 and Period 7 of Day 2.

Table 7.3 Day 1/Day 2 Lunch Schedule

Periods	Specific Times	Number of Class Minutes
1 and 5	8:00–9:30	90 minutes
2 and 6	9:35–11:05	90 minutes
3 and 7	11:10–1:10 (includes lunch)	120 minutes
4 and 8	1:15–2:45	90 minutes

Within periods 3 and 7 of the day 1/day 2 schedule, several options exist.

Table 7.4 Day 1/Day 2 Lunch Options

Minutes	Minutes	Minutes	Minutes
Lunch 30	Class 30	Class 60	Class 90
	Lunch 30	Lunch 30	
Class 90	Class 60	Class 30	Lunch 30

Step 6: Formulate the Core Program of Studies

A key factor in determining the FTE needed in each school, the program of studies details the courses that students will take in each grade. Without prior formulation of this step, a schedule cannot be created. Core courses include reading/language arts, mathematics, social studies, and science; ancillary courses could be world language, technology, STEM, or art. In order to achieve maximum flexibility, the number of instructional periods per day or week cannot exceed the number of periods a teacher is contractually permitted to teach.

Option 1 depicted in Table 7.5 illustrates a program in which teachers may teach six periods per day or 30 periods per week. The school day consists of eight periods plus lunch as a full period or module. If the teaching contract permits, the flex/advisory/intervention period could be added.

Table 7.5 Program of Studies for Core Classes: Option 1

Grade 6		Grade 7		Grade 8	
Course	Periods per Week	Course	Periods per Week	Course	Periods per Week
Reading/ Language Arts	10.0	Reading/ Language Arts	10.0	Reading/ Language Arts	10.0
Social Studies	5.0	Social Studies	5.0	Social Studies	5.0
Mathematics	10.0	Mathematics	10.0	Mathematics	10.0
Science	5.0	Science	5.0	Science	5.0
Total Core	30	Total Core	30	Total Core	30

In option 2, teachers teach five periods per day or 25 periods per week. In this case, the school day consists of seven or eight periods plus a period or module for lunch.

Table 7.6 Program of Studies for Core Classes: Option 2

Grade 6		Grade 7		Grade 8	
Course	Periods per Week	Course	Periods per Week	Course	Periods per Week
Reading/ Language Arts	10.0	Reading/ Language Arts	5.0	Reading/ Language Arts	5.0
Social Studies	5.0	Social Studies	5.0	Social Studies	5.0
Mathematics	5.0	Mathematics	5.0	Algebra I or Mathematics 8	5.0
Science	5.0	Science	5.0	Science	5.0
		Technology/ Art	5.0	Spanish, French or Chinese I	5.0
Total Core	25	Total Core	25	Total Core	25

A flex/advisory/intervention period can be added to courses in both options. While in option 1 the courses and periods per week are similar in all three grades, option 2 suggests a variance from grade to grade. For example, option 2 includes a semester of art and a semester of technology in grade 7. Consequently, teachers from both those subjects attend the interdisciplinary team meetings. In grade 8, Spanish, French, or Chinese I is a required course for all students, providing an integral part for an interdisciplinary approach to instruction.

From a budgeting perspective, the percentage of the day that teachers are with students affects the FTE. The greater the percentage of student contact time results in the need for fewer teachers.

In option 1, teachers teach 75% of the day (six of eight periods). In option 2, teachers teach five of seven periods for 71.4% of the day or five of eight periods for 62.5% of the day. Consequently, the terms of the teachers' contract impact staffing.

Step 7: Formulate the Exploratory/ Elective Program of Studies

In the pioneering days of middle school, the innovators recognized the importance of exploration in learning, especially at this developmental age. Therefore, they determined to provide young adolescent students with opportunities to explore areas outside of what is still considered to be the core curriculum. In this portion of the schedule, opportunities exist for electives as well as required courses. Although many exploratory and elective courses are similar in schools, some may differ according to the culture and need of the community. Typical courses include physical education, art, band, chorus, orchestra, general music, world languages, health, technology, and family and consumer science. Agriculture and financial literacy are examples of outlying courses.

Tier 3 intervention, special education support, and ELL supplements may be part of this portion of the schedule. It is recommended, however, to keep the requirement of least restrictive environment available for all students. As a result of student options, some middle schools schedule students individually for exploratory/elective courses.

Although the exploratory experience plays an important role for middle grade students, budgeting influences the selection of exploratory/elective courses. A correlation exists between the number of courses offered and the FTEs needed. In some cases, the greater the number of electives offered, the lower the average class size for these courses; consequently, these courses may be more expensive in terms of the FTEs needed.

Table 7.7 Program of Studies for Exploratory/Elective Courses

Course	Weeks per Year
Physical Education	20 or 40
Band	20
Chorus	20
Orchestra	20
Tier 3 Math	20
Tier 3 Reading	20
Technology	20
ELL or Special Education Support	20 or 40
World Languages	20 or 40
Art	10
Music	10
Family and Consumer Science	10
Health	10
STEM	10
Financial Literacy	10
Computers	10
Web Page Design	10
Guitar	10
Agriculture	10

If the school offers exploratory/elective courses two periods per day, 80 weeks becomes the guiding number to select from the menu.

If three periods a day, 120 weeks becomes the guiding number. The number of exploratory/elective course periods offered determines the number of teachers needed. Schools/districts desirous of smaller core class sizes limit the opportunity for exploratory/elective experiences. Certain courses may be required each year or a student may need a certain number of weeks in a course for their middle school experience.

Step 8: Project Enrollment

Complementing the selected frameworks and program of studies, the projected enrollment is key to identifying the FTE needed for the school year. This step determines the number of sections at each grade level and the teaming options possible. Local school factors can impact the team configuration decisions.

Grade 6 teaming options need to focus on the students' need in the transition from an elementary school schedule or environment. In Table 7.8, grade 6 could be organized as four two-teacher teams or two four-teacher teams. In grade 7, different configurations for the 10 sections can exist: two five-member teams or two four-teacher teams and one two-teacher team. The most likely arrangement in grade 8 is two five-teacher teams.

The number of core teachers should equal the number of core sections created in grades 6, 7, and 8. This number excludes special education and ELL staff.

Table 7.8 Projected Enrollment and Teaming Options

Grade	Enrollment	Sections	Average Class Size	Team Option
6	200	8	25.0	2 2 2 2 4 4
7	230	10	23.0	4 4 2 5 5
8	250	10	25.0	5 5

Step 9: Decide Team Composition

After analyzing projected enrollment figures, select a teaming option that best meets student needs by focusing on student achievement and subject matter. In Table 7.9, two configurations provide opportunities for double English and double math with an interdisciplinary-maximum flexibility insert.

Table 7.9 Team Composition

Two core teachers plus a Special Education or ELL teacher: • Language Arts, Social Studies, Reading • Mathematics, Science, Reading • Special Education, ELL	Three core teachers plus a Special Education or ELL teacher: • Language Arts/Reading + Social Studies • Language Arts/Reading + Mathematics • Language Arts/Reading + Science • Special Education, ELL
Four core teachers plus a Special Education or ELL teacher: • Language Arts • Social Studies • Mathematics • Science • Special Education, ELL	Four core teachers plus a Special Education or ELL teacher: • Language Arts + Flex/Advisory/Intervention • Social Studies + Flex/Advisory/Intervention • Mathematics + Flex/Advisory/Intervention • Science + Flex/Advisory/Intervention • Special Education, ELL + Flex/Advisory/Intervention
Five core teachers plus a Special Education or ELL teacher: • Language Arts • Social Studies • Mathematics • Science • World Language • Special Education, ELL	Six core teachers plus a Special Education or ELL teacher: • Language Arts/Reading 1 • Mathematics 1 • Social Studies • Science • Language Arts/Reading 2 • Mathematics 2 • Special Education, ELL

Step 10: Develop a Blueprint

Completion of all the previous steps impacts the blueprint, a preliminary design of the master schedule. It reflects the conclusions made about the primary framework and inserts, bell and lunch schedules, core and exploratory/elective program of studies, projected enrollment, and teaming options. On the blueprint, core, exploratory/elective, and lunch are strategically placed. Their placement sets the stage for extended-time periods and the resulting flexibility. In a traditional schedule, teachers benefit from the greatest number of consecutive periods. Interdisciplinary and subject-area or data meetings occur when students are in exploratory/elective classes. Therefore, the capacity of exploratory/elective classes must equal the number of students scheduled from the core sections or teams.

In the traditional blueprint, Table 7.10, the schedule features an 8-period day with lunch as a module of time. The day 1/day 2 blueprint, Table 7.11, presents classes that meet on an alternate day basis. Lunch is a module during periods 3 and 7. As an option, the exploratory/elective classes could meet for 40 minutes daily in the day 1/day 2 schedule.

Table 7.10 Blueprint for a Traditional Schedule

Period	Grade 6	Grade 7	Grade 8
1	Core	Exploratory/Elective	Core
2	Core	Exploratory/Elective	Core
3	Core	Core	Core
4	Core	Core	Core
5	Exploratory/Elective	Core	Core
6	Exploratory/Elective	Core	Core
7	Core	Core	Exploratory/Elective
8	Core	Core	Exploratory/Elective
Lunch between:	5 and 6	6 and 7	4 and 5

Table 7.11 Blueprint for a Day 1/Day 2 Schedule

	Period	Grade 6	Grade 7	Grade 8
Day 1	1	Core	Exploratory/Elective	Core
	2	Exploratory/Elective	Core	Core
	3	Core	Core	Core
	4	Core	Core	Exploratory/Elective
Day 2	5	Core	Exploratory/Elective	Core
	6	Exploratory/Elective	Core	Core
	7	Core	Core	Core
	8	Core	Core	Exploratory/Elective

When the blueprint is completed, the grid of teachers' assignments or master schedule can begin.

Step 11: Assemble the Grid of Teachers' Assignments

Evolving from the blueprint, the grid of teachers' assignments allows the visualization of each teacher's assignment and, ultimately, the actual number of FTEs. Unlike a typical secondary schedule, assignments are organized by teams: 6A, 6B, 7A, 7B, 8A, 8B, and exploratory/elective. Classes do not travel together as cohorts. Students are scheduled on an individual basis using a team or house control number and with sections numbered as in the computer.

In the examples, Tables 7.12a, b, c, and d, and Tables 7.13a, b, c, and d, the following codes are used:

CT = Co-taught class

Repl = A student is in a special education section of a course taught by a special education teacher.

Flex/Adv/I = Flex/advisory/intervention period in which the core teachers control time, provide additional support, cooperate with counselors to present an advisory program, and/or allow time for Tier 2 and Tier 3 instruction.

6/6 = Classes meet on alternate day basis.

7777 = Classes meet daily for ¼ of the school year.

8 = Class meets daily for the year.

Blank cells indicate part-time status.

The following tables separate each grade level and the exploratory/ elective schedule.

Table 7.12a Grid of Teachers' Assignments in a Traditional 8-Period Day

Team	Subject	1	2	3	4	5	6	7	8
6A	R/LA	01 CT	01 CT	02R	TM/DM	Plan	Flex/Adv/I	04 CT	04 CT
	R/LA	02 LA	03	03	TM/DM	Plan	Flex/Adv/I	05	05
	SS	03	04	05	TM/DM	Plan	Flex/Adv/I	01	02
	Math	04	05	01 CT	TM/DM	Plan	Flex/Adv/I	02	03
	Science	05	02	04	TM/DM	Plan	Flex/Adv/I	03	01
	Sp. Ed.	Eng. CT	Eng. CT	Math CT	TM/DM	Plan	Flex/Adv/I	Eng. CT	Eng. CT
	ELL				TM/DM		Flex/Adv/I		
6B	R/LA	06	06	07R	TM/DM	Plan	Flex/Adv/I	09	09
	R/LA	07 LA	08	08	TM/DM	Plan	Flex/Adv/I	10	10
	SS	08	09	10	TM/DM	Plan	Flex/Adv/I	06	07
	Math	09	10	06	TM/DM	Plan	Flex/Adv/I	07	08
	Science	10	07	09	TM/DM	Plan	Flex/Adv/I	08	06
Lunch is between periods 3 and 4									

Table 7.12b Grid of Teachers' Assignments in a Traditional 8-Period Day

Team	Subject	1	2	3	4	5	6	7	8
7A	R/LA	TM/DM	Plan	H01	01	02CT	03	04CT	Flex/Adv/I
	SS	TM/DM	Plan	01	02	03	04	05	Flex/Adv/I
	Math	TM/DM	Plan	01CT	02	Alg. I 01	03	04	Flex/Adv/I
	Science	TM/DM	Plan	01	02	03	04	05	Flex/Adv/I
	Tech/Art	TM/DM	Plan	01	02	03	04	05	Flex/Adv/I
	Sp. Ed.	TM/DM	Plan	Math CT		Eng. CT		Eng. CT	Flex/Adv/I
	ELL	TM/DM							Flex/Adv/I
7B	R/LA	TM/DM	Plan	05	H 02	06	07	08	Flex/Adv/I
	SS	TM/DM	Plan	06	07	08	09	10	Flex/Adv/I
	Math	TM/DM	Plan	05	06	07	Alg. I 02	08	Flex/Adv/I
	Science	TM/DM	Plan	06	07	08	09	10	Flex/Adv/I
	Tech/Art	TM/DM	Plan	06	07	08	09	10	Flex/Adv/I
Lunch is between periods 5 and 6									

Table 7.12c Grid of Teachers' Assignments in a Traditional 8-Period Day

Team	Subject	1	2	3	4	5	6	7	8
8A	R/LA	01 CT	H 01	02 CT	Flex/Adv/I	03	04	TM/DM	Plan
	SS	01	02	03	Flex/Adv/I	04 CT	05	TM/DM	Plan
	Math	Alg. I 01	M 8 01 CT	Alg. II 01	Flex/Adv/I	Alg. I 02	M 8 02	TM/DM	Plan
	Science	01	02	03	Flex/Adv/I	04	05	TM/DM	Plan
	Spanish	01	02	03	Flex/Adv/I	04	05	TM/DM	Plan

Continued

Table 7.12c Continued

	Sp. Ed.	Eng. CT	Math CT	Eng. CT	Flex/Adv/I	Alg. I CT	Math Repl.	TM/DM	Plan
	ELL				Flex/Adv/I			TM/DM	
8B	R/LA	05	H 02	06	Flex/Adv/I	07	H 03	TM/DM	Plan
	SS	06	07	08	Flex/Adv/I	09	10	TM/DM	Plan
	Math	Alg. I 03	M8 03	M8 04	Flex/Adv/I	Alg. II 02	Alg. I 04	TM/DM	Plan
	Sci.	06	07	08	Flex/Adv/I	09	10	TM/DM	Plan
	Spanish	06	07	08	Flex/Adv/I	09	10	TM/DM	Plan

Lunch is between periods 4 and 5

Table 7.12d Grid of Teachers' Assignments in a Traditional 8-Period Day

Explo./Elect.	Subject	1	2	3	4	5	6	7	8
	PE 1	7 / 7	7 / 7	TM/DM	6 / 6	6 / 6	Plan	8 / 8	
	PE 2	7 / 7		TM/DM	6 / 6	6 / 6	Plan	8 / 8	8 / 8
	PE 3	7 / 7	7 / 7	TM/DM	6 / 6		Plan	8 / 8	8 / 8
	FCS	7 7 7 7	7 7 7 7	TM/DM	6 6 6 6	6 6 6 6	Plan	8 / 8	8 / 8
	Tier 3 Math	7 / 7	7 / 7	TM/DM	6 / 6	6 / 6	Plan	8 / 8	8 / 8
	Tier 3 Rdg.	7 / 7	7 / 7	TM/DM	6 / 6	6 / 6	Plan	8 / 8	8 / 8
	Computer	7 7 7 7	7 7 7 7	TM/DM	6 6 6 6	6 6 6 6	Plan	8 / 8	8 / 8
	Band	7 / 7		TM/DM	6 / 6	6 / 6	Plan	8	8 / 8

Continued

Explo./Elect.	Subject	1	2	3	4	5	6	7	8
	Orchestra		7 / 7	TM/DM		6 / 6	Plan	8 / 8	8
	Chorus	7 / 7	7 / 7	TM/DM	6 / 6	6 / 6	Plan	8 / 8	8 / 8
	Art			TM/DM	6 6 / 6 6	6 6 / 6 6	Plan	8 / 8	8 / 8
	Sp. Ed. Support	7 / 7	7 / 7	TM/DM	6 / 6	6 / 6	Plan	8 / 8	8 / 8
	ELL Support	7 / 7	7 / 7	TM/DM	6 / 6	6 / 6	Plan	8 / 8	8 / 8
	Music—6 Guitar—7 & 8	7 7 / 7 7	7 7 / 7 7	TM/DM	6 6 / 6 6	6 6 / 6 6	Plan	8 / 8	8 / 8
	World Language	7 7 / 7 7	7 7 / 7 7	TM/DM	6 6 / 6 6	6 6 / 6 6	Plan		
Lunch is between periods 3 and 4									

Table 7.13a Grid of Teachers' Assignments in a Day 1/Day 2 Schedule: Lunch Is a Module

		Day 1				Day 2			
Team	Subject	1	2	3	4	5	6	7	8
6A	R/LA	01- CT	TM/P	H-01	02	03	DM/P	04-CT	Flex/Adv./I
	STEM	01	TM/P	02	03	04	DM/P	05	Flex/Adv./I
	SS	01	TM/P	02	03	04	DM/P	05	Flex/Adv./I
	Math	H-01	TM/P	01 CT	02	03 CT	DM/P	04	Flex/Adv./I
	Science	01	TM/P	02	03	04	DM/P	05	Flex/Adv./I
	Sp. Ed.	Eng.-CT	TM/P	Math-CT		Math-CT	DM/P	Eng.-CT	Flex/Adv./I

Continued

Table 7.13a Continued

Team	Subject	Day 1				Day 2			
		1	2	3	4	5	6	7	8
	ELL		TM/P				DM/P		Flex/Adv./I
6B	R/LA	05	TM/P	H-02	06	07	DM/P	08	Flex/Adv./I
	STEM	06	TM/P	07	08	09	DM/P	10	Flex/Adv./I
	SS	06	TM/P	07	08	09	DM/P	10	Flex/Adv./I
	Math	05	TM/P	06	07	H-02	DM/P	08	Flex/Adv./I
	Science	06	TM/P	07	08	09	DM/P	10	Flex/Adv./I

Table 7.13b Grid of Teachers' Assignments in a
Day 1/Day 2 Schedule: Lunch Is a Module

Team	Subject	Day 1				Day 2			
		1	2	3	4	5	6	7	8
7A	R/LA	TM/P	H-01	01	Flex/Adv./I	DM/P	02 CT	03	04 CT
	SS	TM/P	01	02	Flex/Adv./I	DM/P	03	04	05
	Math	TM/P	01-CT	02	Flex/Adv./I	DM/P	Alg.I-01	03	04
	Science	TM/P	01	02	Flex/Adv./I	DM/P	03	04	05
	Art/Tech	TM/P	01	02	Flex/Adv./I	DM/P	03	04	05
	Sp. Ed.	TM/P	Math CT	Repl. Math	Flex/Adv./I	DM/P	Eng. CT	Repl. Math	Eng. CT
	ELL	TM/P			Flex/Adv./I	DM/P			
7B	R/LA	TM/P	05	H-02	Flex/Adv./I	DM/P	06	07	08
	SS	TM/P	06	07	Flex/Adv./I	DM/P	08	09	10

Continued

Team	Subject	Day 1				Day 2			
		1	2	3	4	5	6	7	8
	Math	TM/P	05	06	Flex/Adv./I	DM/P	07	Alg. I-02	08
	Science	TM/P	06	07	Flex/Adv./I	DM/P	08	09	10
	Tech/Art	TM/P	06	07	Flex/Adv./I	DM/P	08	09	10

Table 7.13c Grid of Teachers' Assignments in a
Day 1/Day 2 Schedule: Lunch Is a Module

Team	Subject	Day 1				Day 2			
		1	2	3	4	5	6	7	8
8A	R/LA	01-CT	H-01	02-CT	TM/P	03	04	Flex/Adv./I	DM/P
	SS	01	02	03	TM/P	04	05	Flex/Adv./I	DM/P
	Math	Alg. I-01	M8–01 CT	Alg. II–01	TM/P	Alg. I-02 CT	M8–02	Flex/Adv./I	DM/P
	Science	01	02	03	TM/P	04	05	Flex/Adv./I	DM/P
	Spanish	01	02	03	TM/P	04	05	Flex/Adv./I	DM/P
	Sp. Ed.	Eng. CT	M8 CT	Eng. CT	TM/P	Alg. I CT	Repl. Math	Flex/Adv./I	DM/P
	ELL				TM/P			Flex/Adv./I	DM/P
8B	R/LA	05	H-02	06	TM/P	07	H-03	Flex/Adv./I	DM/P
	SS	06	07	08	TM/P	09	10	Flex/Adv./I	DM/P
	Math	Alg. I-03	M8–03	M8–04	TM/P	Alg. II-02	Alg. I-04	Flex/Adv./I	DM/P
	Sci.	06	07	08	TM/P	09	10	Flex/Adv./I	DM/P
	Spanish	06	07	08	TM/P	09	10	Flex/Adv./I	DM/P

Table 7.13d Grid of Teachers' Assignments in a
Day 1/Day 2 Schedule: Lunch Is a Module

Subject	Day 1				Day 2			
	1	2	3	4	5	6	7	8
PE 1	7 / 7	6 / 6	TM/P	8 / 8	7 / 7	6 / 6	DM/P	8 / 8
PE 2	7 / 7	6 / 6	TM/P	8 / 8	7 / 7	6 / 6	DM/P	8 / 8
PE 3	7 / 7	6 / 6	TM/P	8 / 8				
FCS	7 7 7 7	6 6 6 6	TM/P	8 / 8	7 7 7 7	6 6 6 6	DM/P	8 / 8
Tier 3 Math	7 / 7	6 / 6	TM/P	8 / 8	7 / 7	6 / 6	DM/P	8 / 8
Tier 3 Rdg.	7 / 7	6 / 6	TM/P	8 / 8	7 / 7	6 / 6	DM/P	8 / 8
Computer	7 7 7 7	6 6 6 6	TM/P	8 / 8	7 7 7 7	6 6 6 6	DM/P	8 / 8
Band	7 / 7	6 / 6	TM/P	8	7 / 7	6 / 6	DM/P	
Orchestra		6 / 6	TM/P		7 / 7	6 / 6	DM/P	8
Chorus	7 / 7	6 / 6	TM/P	8 / 8	7 / 7	6 / 6	DM/P	8 / 8
Art		6 6 6 6	TM/P	8 / 8		6 6 6 6	DM/P	8 / 8
Sp. Ed. Support	7 / 7	6 / 6	TM/P	8 / 8	7 / 7	6 / 6	DM/P	8 / 8
ELL Support	7 / 7	6 / 6	TM/P	8 / 8	7 / 7	6 / 6	DM/P	8 / 8
Music—6 Guitar—7 & 8	7 7 7 7	6 6 6 6	TM/P	8 / 8	7 7 7 7	6 6 6 6	DM/P	8 / 8
World Language	7 7 7 7	6 6 6 6	TM/P		7 7 7 7	6 6 6 6	DM/P	

When the grid of assignments is completed, the actual number of FTEs is verified.

Step 12: Implement Professional Development

Professional development sets the stage for teacher ownership as well as an effective and equitable schedule. Most successful when implemented as an ongoing process, professional development content should include strategies for advisory, RtI, role and function of teams, and teaching in extended-time periods.

Recap

The design and implementation of the master schedule reinforce the middle school concept. The step-by-step process described in this chapter enables educational leaders to achieve these objectives. The primary objective of the schedule is to address the unique needs of early adolescent learners. Traditionally, the middle school schedules differ from high school models developed in Chapter 8. More recently, high school schedules extend component parts of the middle school concept in grades 9–12.

Points to Consider

1. How has the mission/vision statement guided the work in building the schedule?

2. In developing the schedule, how did the committee gain faculty understanding and support?

3. In what ways does the schedule facilitate an understanding of and support for the benefits of the middle school concept?

4. How does the schedule enable teachers to implement the three tiers of RtI?

5. Describe ways the committee reviewed primary frameworks and inserts in terms of student needs?

6. How does the master schedule introduce an interdisciplinary team structure that accommodates subject matter specialization?

7. Describe how the committee used the projected enrollment to explore teaming options.

8. How does the schedule accommodate the program of studies?

9. Confirm that opportunities exist for all students to participate in the elective program.

10. Affirm that the number of exploratory/elective teachers allows for common planning time for core teachers.

11. Is common planning time provided for exploratory/elective teachers?

12. Confirm that the blueprint set the stage for extended-time periods in core classes.

13. How does the schedule meet the needs of a diverse population?

14. Confirm that the schedule provides the least restrictive environment for all students.

15. How does the professional development program encourage teachers to take ownership of the schedule?

16. How does the professional program provide training to maximize opportunities for flexibility?

17. To what extent are schedules within the district consistent with each other?

Steps in Building a High School Schedule

Focus

- Nineteen steps to build a high school master schedule
- Tables and examples illustrate steps

A high school schedule incorporates a variety of considerations such as Advanced Placement classes, freshman academies, and multiple elective offerings. The following 19 steps address the complexities and provide clear directions on providing an efficient and equitable schedule for staff and students.

Step 1: Review, Revise, or Create the Mission/Vision Statement

As in a classroom where target learning guides the instruction, the mission/vision statement serves as the target for decision-making. This is no less true in seeking an efficient and equitable schedule than in seeking the curriculum and programs that best meet the needs of the students to be served. The statement influences the desired outcomes of specific features applied to the schedule as well as all facets within the school day for the high school experience. It exists as the foundation for a contemporary high school in the context and culture of the school and community.

Step 2: Gain Faculty Understanding and Support

Any decision that affects faculty and must be implemented by them benefits from their expertise. During scheduling discussions, aspects of scheduling require understanding by all involved staff. Those aspects include the purpose of the schedule, the operation of small learning communities, career pathways, collaboration, intervention, and flexibility to implement the high school schedule. The resulting knowledge base of the faculty prepares them to explain the approved schedule to students, parents, board of education members, and the community. In the teachers' preparation, the principal informs and encourages them to use the schedule in their daily decision-making.

Step 3: Prepare for the Three Tiers of RtI

RtI philosophies and practice in the district need to be in place and understood by all stakeholders. Tier 1 interventions are best accomplished by providing opportunities for learning through implementation of extended-time periods for the classroom, which appear in primary and insert frameworks discussed in step 4. Tier 2 interventions are best met when the schedule provides an intervention/enrichment period often in the form of a flex/advisory/intervention period. This period can exist school-wide or as an element of a freshman academy, career pathways, or other magnet or academy formats. To meet students' specific RtI needs, grade-level teachers explore scheduling designs for the implementation of that intervention/enrichment period.

During common planning time, teachers make decisions about placement and levels of RtI relying on student data and feedback from all teachers and support staff. In part, their decisions need to assure the fluidity of movement for students within the Tier 2 and 3 designations. As students make course selections for the next school year, an option for Tier 3 mathematics or reading needs to be in place. These courses will be part of the course requests in the registration process.

Step 4: Choose Primary Framework and Inserts

When choosing the primary framework and inserts, the committee consistently uses the mission/vision statement to guide decisions. Primary frameworks to be considered include the traditional 6-, 7-, 8-, or 9-period day; semester 1/semester 2; day 1/day 2; and trimester. Once the primary framework is chosen, the fulfillment of delivering the curriculum influences the choice of inserts. Inserts frequently chosen include double English/double math, single-subject teams, interdisciplinary-maximum or limited flexibility teams, interdisciplinary exploratory/elective teams, credit recovery, or combination teams. Since few inserts are mutually exclusive, multiple inserts can be included within the master schedule. In order to ensure successful implementation, the faculty needs to provide input on decisions. After decisions are made, successful implementation requires professional development that addresses effective implementation of the schedule.

Primary Frameworks

- Traditional 6-, 7-, 8-, or 9-Period Day
- Day 1/Day 2
- Semester 1/Semester 2
- Trimester

Inserts

- Double English/Double Math

- Single-Subject Team

- Interdisciplinary-Maximum Flexibility Team

- Interdisciplinary-Limited Flexibility Team

- Interdisciplinary Exploratory/Elective Team

- Combination Team

- Credit Recovery

- Rotational

Step 5: Create Bell and Lunch Schedule

While the teachers' contract may determine the length of the lunch period, the primary framework determines placement of the bell and lunch schedules. In a traditional schedule, lunch can be a full period or a 30/35-minute module. Modular lunch schedules increase instructional time.

Table 8.1 Traditional Lunch Schedule

Full Period	Period	Time
	1	8:00–8:45
	2	8:45–9:30
	3	9:30–10:15
Lunch	4	10:15–11:00
Lunch	5	11:00–11:45
Lunch	6	11:45–12:30
	7	12:30–1:15
	8	1:15–2:00
	9	2:00–2:45

Table 8.2 Modular Lunch Schedule

			Period	Mod	Time			
			1	(1)	8:00–8:45			
			2	(2)	8:50–9:35			
			3	(3)	9:40–10:25			
A			B			C		
Period	Mod	Time	Period	Mod	Time	Period	Mod	Time
Lunch	(4)	10:25–10:55	4	(4–5)	10:30–11:15	4	(4–5)	10:30–11:15
4	(5–6)	11:00–11:45	Lunch	(6)	11:15–11:45	5	(6–7)	11:20–12:05
5	(7–8)	11:50–12:35	5	(7–8)	11:50–12:35	Lunch	(8)	12:05–12:35
			6	(9)	12:40–1:25			
			7	(10)	1:30–2:15			
			8	(11)	2:20–3:05			

In a variation of the modular model, the lunch periods for semester 1/semester 2 and day 1/day 2 are embedded in periods 3 and 7.

Table 8.3 Modular Lunch Schedule for Semester 1/Semester 2 or Day 1/Day 2

Periods	Specific Times	Number of Class Minutes
1 and 5	8:00–9:30	90 minutes
2 and 6	9:35–11:05	90 minutes
3 and 7	11:10–1:10 (includes lunch)	120 minutes
4 and 8	1:15–2:45	90 minutes

Within periods 3 and 7, several options exist.

Table 8.4 Options for Semester 1/Semester 2
or Day 1/Day 2 Modular Lunch

Minutes	Minutes	Minutes	Minutes
Lunch 30	Class 30	Class 60	Class 90
	Lunch 30	Lunch 30	
Class 90	Class 60	Class 30	Lunch 30

In the trimester framework, schools use the following bell/lunch schedule.

Table 8.5 Trimester Lunch Schedule

Minutes	Specific Times	Trimester I	Trimester 2	Trimester 3
		Period	Period	Period
72	8:00–9:12	1	6	11
72	9:17–10:29	2	7	12
72 + 30	10:34–12:16	3	8	13
72	12:21–1:33	4	9	14
72	1:38–2:50	5	10	15

Table 8.6 Trimester Lunch Schedule Periods
3, 8, and 13: Distribution of 102 Minutes

Minutes	Minutes	Minutes
Lunch 30	Class 30	Class 72
	Lunch 30	
Class 72	Class 42	Lunch 30

Step 6: Decisions on Composition of Houses, Magnets, and Academies

Prior to preparing the curriculum handbook and registration materials, the composition of small learning communities needs to be made. A digit added to the course number reflects a course required by a specific small learning community.

Step 7: Review and/or Update Curriculum Handbook for Students and Parents

As the mission/vision statement guides scheduling decisions, so does the curriculum handbook reflect that statement. Prior to any reform or creation of a schedule, the curriculum handbook needs to be current. Today, this information often appears online for students and parents. The handbook typically contains the core curriculum, graduation requirements, elective offerings as well as details about freshman academy, magnets, and career pathways programs.

Table 8.7 Course Requests: Traditional 8-Period Day, Semester 1/Semester 2, or Day 1/Day2

Course	Course Number
English 10	1010
Global Studies	2010
Geometry	3030
Chemistry	4050
French III	6042
Physical Education/Health	8060
Band	5306
Animation	8092

Table 8.8 Course Requests: Trimesters

Course	Course Number	Course	Course Number
English 10B—Credit Recovery	1011	Algebra II B	3033
		Chemistry A	4050
English 11A	1100	Chemistry B	4051
English 11B	1101	French II A	6040
US History A	2020	French II B	6041
US History B	2021	Physical Education A	8060
Geometry 10B—Credit Recovery	3030		
		Art II B	7201
Algebra II A	3032	Art III A	7300

Step 8: Assemble Registration Materials and Coordinate Course Selection Process

The procedure for students to select specific courses can exist as either an online process or the traditional paper form. A process of teacher approval for the selection of some courses needs to be in place. When the enrollment is completed, a count for the total number of students requesting each course is determined.

Step 9: Establish Student Data Base

Immediately after the course selection or registration process is completed, a student data base emerges, reflecting the numbers of all courses requested. At this point, the data base becomes a managerial tool for administrators and counselors but not the official tally or basis for determining the number of sections of courses. Of importance, the course numbering reflects specific courses and programs such as career pathways, house, magnets, or academies. At the end of the school year and periodically throughout the summer, the data base needs to be revisited to reflect enrollment and other changes to provide a solid base on which to monitor course section decisions.

Table 8.9 Data Base Example

Student	ID #	1	2	3	4	5	6	7	8
King, Sally	568237	1010	2010	3010	4010	5070	7846	8642	9375
Chavez, Tony	610029	1031	2039	3620	4178	5119	0151	7161	1378
Oskar, Tara	413862	1411	2893	3421	4998	5683	3629	4198	8642

Step 10: Create Department Summaries

A vital managerial strategy, the department summary enables equitable distribution of staff in a school and district. Based on student requests, the tally for each department is a starting point for staffing. As retentions, new entrants, and withdrawals occur, adjustments will be needed. A portion of the summary for the mathematics department follows.

Table 8.10 Mathematics Department Summary

Course	Enrollment	Sections	Average Class Size	Weight	Aggregate Periods
H Algebra I	53	2	26.5	5	10
Algebra I	93	4	23.3	5	20
CT Algebra I	16	(3)	(5.3)	—	—
H Geometry	112	4	28.0	5	20
Geometry	200	8	25.0	5	40
CT Geometry	36	(5)	(7.2)	—	—
Tier 3 Math	46	7	6.6	2.5	17.5
H Algebra II	100	4	25.0	5	20
Algebra II	215	9	23.9	5	45
CT Algebra II	50	(9)	(5.6)	—	—
Total					**172.5**
					Divided by 30 = 5.75 teachers
					Divided by 25 = 6.9 teachers

An explanation of each column follows:

- Student request tally provides *enrollment* information for each course.

- *Sections* identifies the number to meet the desired average class size.

- If a section needs to be added or deleted, *average class size* facilitates those decisions.

- *Weighting* calculates the valence or relative value of a specific course in a department and in the district budget.

  - A course meeting the equivalent of five periods a week for the year receives a weighting of 5.

  - Courses that meet every other day for the year or every day for one semester each receive a weighting of 2.5.

  - Courses that meet the equivalent of two periods per day for the year each have a weight of 10.

- To calculate *aggregate periods* per course, multiply the number of sections by the weight of the course, e.g. eight sections of geometry at a weight of 5 equals 40 aggregate periods. The final calculations result in the total aggregate periods for a department and the number of teachers needed for that department.

A direct correlation exists between the number of periods a teacher can teach per week and the number of FTEs needed for that department. If the teachers' contract allows 30 periods of student contact teaching per week, the FTEs needed are fewer than a contract in which 25 periods of student contact teaching are allowed. The lower right corner of Table 8.10 indicates the total aggregate periods for that department and the FTE needed: 5.75 teachers for the 30-periods-per-week teacher and 6.9 teachers for the 25-periods-per-week teacher.

In the enrollment column, Algebra I CT and Geometry CT reflect the number of special education students whose IEP calls for a co-taught setting. These students are included in the count. The 16 students in Algebra I CT and 36 students in Geometry CT are distributed among existing sections, three sections of Algebra I and five sections of Geometry. In these courses, special and general education teachers work collaboratively. CT teachers are included in the special education department summary.

If a trimester schedule is in place, the weight column is not needed. Adding the number of sections and dividing by 12 yields the FTE needed for a department. Calculating the department summary for a trimester schedule involves listing each course separately, e.g., Algebra I A and Algebra I B. In the case of band, the listing appears as Band A, Band B, Band C. A one-trimester course is just Art I A.

Table 8.11 Mathematics Department Summary for Trimesters

Course	Enrollment	Sections	Average Class Size
H Algebra I A	53	2	26.5
Algebra I A	93	4	23.3
CT Algebra I A	16	(3)	(5.3)
H Geometry A	112	4	28.0
Geometry A	200	8	25.0
CT Geometry A	36	(5)	(7.2)
Tier III Math A	46	7	6.6
H Algebra II A	100	4	25.0
Algebra II A	215	9	23.9
CT Algebra II A	50	(9)	(5.6)
Total		**38**	

Step 11: Create the FTE Distribution Table

While the department summary identifies sections needed for a course, the FTE distribution table indicates the distribution of available staff by department. Occasionally, the number of FTEs desired exceeds the FTE provided to the school. When that occurs, principals reduce the number of sections in courses with the lowest average class size. Another reduction option eliminates elective offerings with limited enrollment. In both cases, the decisions seek equity. After the completion of department summaries and teacher assignments charts, the exact number of FTEs is officially confirmed.

Table 8.12 High School FTE Distribution Chart

Department	FTE Requested
English	9.5
Social Studies	8.0
Mathematics	10.0
Science	9.0
World Language	6.0
Business	4.5
Physical Education	4.75
Art	3.0
Music	3.0
Agriculture	2.7
Total	**60.45**

Step 12: Create Teacher Assignment Chart

Following the determination of allocated FTEs, configuring the specific assignments for teachers begins. At the outset, assign teachers within the small learning communities—magnets, houses, and academies.

Again, equity drives the process by monitoring average daily student loads per teacher.

Table 8.13 Sample Teacher Assignment Chart

Teacher	Assignment	Aggregate Periods	Full Time Equivalent (FTE)	Average Daily Student Load
#1	4 Algebra I (20) 2 Algebra II (10)	30	1.0	165
#2	2 Algebra II (10) 2 H Algebra I (10) 1 Algebra I (5)	25	1.0	145
#3	4 Geometry (20) 1 H Geometry (5)	25	1.0	150

Table 8.14 Trimester Teacher Assignment Chart

Teacher	Assignment
#1	6 English 9A 6 English 9B = 12 (Freshman Academy)
#2	3 Spanish IIA 3 Spanish IIB 3 Spanish IIIA 3 Spanish IIIB = 12 (International Studies Career Pathway)
#3	3 FCS IA 3 FCS IB 3 FCS 2A 3 FCS 2B = 12 (Human Growth and Development Academy)
#4	6 Art IA 6 Art IB = 12

Step 13: List Singletons and Doubletons

Singleton and doubleton courses are determined by a review of the department summaries. A singleton identifies a one-section offering;

a doubleton identifies a two-section offering. Because the goal of the schedule is to provide opportunities for students to receive their first choice of courses, distribute singletons and doubletons over various periods of the school day. Regardless of the primary framework, this form of distribution maximizes the likelihood that the greatest number of students will receive their first choices. Although the following charts appear identical, they illustrate the importance of creating charts to spread singletons and doubletons in the initial draft of the master schedule.

Table 8.15 Singleton Chart

Course Number	Course Name
1089	AP English 12
3195	Pre-Calculus
4195	AP Biology
4185	AP Chemistry
5192	French V
5142	Spanish V
4200	H Physics
6601	Band
6603	Orchestra
6607	A Capella Chorus

Table 8.16 Doubleton Chart

Course Number	Course Name
2090	AP US Government and Econ.
5155	Spanish IV
5201	French IV
3200	H Algebra II
3205	H Geometry
3104	H English 11
6701	Percussion Ensemble
1936	Tier 3 Reading
3926	Tier 3 Math
5666	German II

Step 14: Formulate a Conflict Matrix for Each Singleton and Doubleton Course

Traditional, Semester 1/Semester 2, and Day 1/Day 2

To continue maximizing students receiving their first choice, patterns of course requests need analysis. These matrices are the managerial tool to effectively spread singletons and doubletons throughout the schedule.

Table 8.17 Singleton Course Matrix: AP English 12

Course #	Course Name	Corresponding Enrollment	# of Sections Available	Period Assigned
1084	AP English 12	18	1	1
2095	AP US Govt. and Economics	15	2	
2090	US Govt. & Economics	3	6	
3195	AP Calculus	13	1	7
3193	Pre-Calculus	5	4	
3185	Probability & Statistics	7	4	
4195	AP Biology	10	1	2
4185	AP Chemistry	8	1	2
5192	French V	4	1	5
5142	Spanish V	14	1	5

To illustrate the importance of spreading each singleton, the above chart indicates periods identified for other courses needed by students enrolled in singleton courses. After completing that listing,

Table 8.18 Segment of Master Schedule Reflecting Spread of
Courses Identified in Conflict Matrix for AP English 12

Period	1	2	3	4	5	6	7	8
	AP English 12–01	AP Biology —01	AP Govt. & Econ. —01		French V —01		AP Calc. —01	AP Govt. & Econ. —02
		AP Chemis- try —01			Span- ish V —01			
	US Govt. & Econ. —01	US Govt. & Econ. —02	US Govt. & Econ. —03	US Govt. & Econ. —04	US Govt. & Econ. —05	US Govt. & Econ. —06		
	Pre- Calc. —01			Pre- Calc. —02			Pre- Calc. —03	Pre- Calc. —04
		Prob. & Stat. —01	Prob. & Stat. —02		Prob.& Stat. —03	Prob. & Stat. —04		

repeat the process for doubletons. Based on the matrix process, Table 8.18 illustrates how the computer assigns students to classes. The table identifies other courses for students in the Honors English 12 singleton course.

Some singletons can be listed at the same time. No student requested both AP Biology and AP Chemistry; therefore, they can be scheduled at the same time. Similarly, French V and Spanish V can be scheduled for the same period. In reality, the confirmation of course placements cannot be finalized until at least the first computer run. Often, many singleton and doubleton courses appear among student course requests.

Trimester Variation of Conflict Matrix

Most courses in a trimester schedule have a double or triple entry, e.g., English 12 becomes English 12A and English 12B. When a full year is required for a course, it has a triple entry, e.g., AP Calculus A, AP Calculus B, and AP Calculus C. When double or triple designations exist, each designation is a separate course.

Table 8.19 Trimester Matrix for Singleton Course: Honors English 11A and 11B

Course #	Course Title	Enrollment	Sections	Period(s)
1015	H English 11A	22	1	8
1016	H English 11B	22	1	11
2020	H US History A	21	1	3
2021	H US History B	21	1	12
3704	AP Calculus A	18	2	2, 4
3705	AP Calculus B	18	2	7, 9
3411	H Algebra II A	3	4	1, 2, 3, 7
3412	H Algebra II B	3	4	8, 9
3300	H Geometry A	1	2	2, 4
3301	H Geometry B	1	2	9, 14
4256	H Physics A	16	1	5
4567	H Physics B	16	1	13
4904	AP Chemistry A	6	2	1, 5
4905	AP Chemistry B	6	2	6, 10
5155	Spanish IV A	10	2	8, 9
5156	Spanish IV B	10	2	14, 15
5201	French IV A	12	2	8, 9
5202	French IV B	12	2	14, 15

Table 8.20 illustrates singletons to highlight the complexity of the trimester scheduling process. Because AP testing occurs in May, AP courses need to be offered in trimesters 1 and 2 or in all three trimesters. As a result, students may be limited on the number of AP courses they may take in a given school year. They need to be aware of the

Table 8.20 Trimester Master Schedule Segment Reflecting Courses Identified in Conflict Matrix for Honors English 11A and 11B

Period	English	Social Studies	Math	Science	Spanish	French
1				AP Chem. A-01		
2			AP Calc. A-01 H Alg. II A-01 H Geo. A 01			
3		H US Hist. A-01	H Geo. A-01 H Alg. II A-02 H Geo. A-02			
4			AP Calc. A-02 H Alg. II A-03			
5				AP Chem. A-02 H Physics A-01		
6				AP Chem. B-01		
7			AP Calc. B-01 H Alg. II B-01			
8	H Eng. 11 A-01		H Alg. II B-01		Sp. IV A-01	Fr. IV A-01
9			AP Calc. B-02 H Alg. II B-02 H Geo. B-01		Sp. IV A-02	Fr. IV A-02

Continued

Period	English	Social Studies	Math	Science	Spanish	French
10				AP Chem. B-02		
11	H Eng. 11 B-01		H Alg. II B-04			
12		H US Hist. B-01				
13				H Physics B-01		
14			H Alg. II B-05 H Geo. B-02		Sp. IV B-01	Fr. IV B-01
15					Sp. IV B-02	Fr. IV B-02

sequence of their chosen AP and honors courses and encouraged to take some AP courses prior to grade 12.

Based on Honors English 11A and B, Table 8.20 demonstrates how a matrix is created for each singleton and doubleton. Note that three doubleton courses cannot be scheduled in the same two periods of the day.

Step 15: Create a Blueprint for Small Learning Communities

Concurrent with the placement of singletons and doubletons on the grid for any of the primary frameworks, create a blueprint for the various small learning communities. The blueprint minimizes the likelihood of tracking caused by the placement of singletons or doubletons in the schedule. A student may need to leave a small learning community or academy for a singleton taught outside of the community or academy.

The blueprint in Table 8.21 illustrates a freshman academy program with four cohorts. The goal of this blueprint is to avoid tracking for any of the academies based on the placement of singleton electives. In this example, no academy classes appear in period 5,

Table 8.21 Sample Blueprint for Freshman Academies

Period	Team 9A	Team 9B	Team 9C	Team 9D
1		Core		Core
2		Core		Core
3	Core	Core	Core	
4	Core	Core	Core	
5				
6	Core		Core	
7	Core		Core	Core
8				Core

allowing students from any academy to be in band, chorus, or orchestra. If placed in period 8, the Mandarin II singleton allows 15 students enrolled to be distributed among three cohorts.

Step 16: Place Singletons and Doubletons on the Master Schedule by Teacher and Period

At this point, placement of singletons and doubletons on the grid of specific teachers' assignments begins. Tables 8.22–8.24 focus on the spread and distribution of singletons and doubletons for each of the primary frameworks according to assignments of specific teachers.

Table 8.22 Place Singletons and Doubletons:
Traditional 9-Period Schedule

Period	1	2	3	4	5	6	7	8	9
Teacher #1	S 1015–01	S 1900–01							
Teacher #2				S 2105–01	S 2107–01				
Teacher #3						S 4617–01			
Teacher #4		D 6262–01		D 6365–01			D 6365–02	D 6262–02	
Teacher #5	D 7902–01		D 7901–01			D 7902–02			D 7901–02

Table 8.23 Place Singletons and Doubletons: Day 1/Day 2
or Semester 1/Semester 2

Period	A1	A2	A3	A4	B1	B2	B3	B4
Teacher #1	S 1015–01	S 1900–01						
Teacher #2				S 2105–01	S 2107–01			
Teacher #3						S 4617–01		
Teacher #4		D 6262–01		D 6365–01		D 6365–02	D 6262–02	
Teacher #5	D 7902–01		D 7901–01		D 7902–02			D 7901–02

Table 8.24 Place Singletons and Doubletons: Trimester Schedule

Period	Trimester #1					Trimester #2					Trimester #3				
	1	2	3	4	5	6	7	8	9	10	11	12	13	14	15
Teacher #1	AP Eng. 12A-01				H Eng. 11A-01	AP Eng. 12B-01		H Eng. 10A-01		H Eng. 11B-01			H Eng. 10B-01		
Teacher #2			AP US A-01			H SS 11A-01		AP US B-01			HSS 11B-01				
Teacher #3					Alg. I A-01	H Alg. I A-01			H Geo. A-01	Alg. I B-01	H Alg. I B-01			H Geo. B-01	Alg. I C-01
Teacher #4	H Bio. A-01												H Bio- B-01		

Step 17: Enter Remainder of Courses

After singletons and doubletons are entered on the grid, place the remaining courses. During this process, several checks are vital:

1. Each teacher's required number of planning periods appears on the grid.
2. Each period has the same number of seats available to distribute students equitably.
3. The same number of sections or seats is available for each grade level each period.
4. Unlike typical high school schedules, small learning communities are entered first.
5. Then each department is listed with remaining FTE members.
6. Continue to use the conflict matrix in decision-making.

Tables 8.25, 8.26, and 8.27 illustrate this step for each of the primary frameworks.

Table 8.25 Enter Remainder of Courses: Traditional 9-Period Day

Period	1	2	3	4	5	6	7	8	9
Teacher #1	S 1015–01	S 1900–01	Plan	1013–04	Lunch	Dept. Mtg.	1013–05	1905–05	1013–06
Teacher #2	Dept. Mtg.	2100–05	Plan	S 2105–01	S 2107–01	Lunch	2100–06	2100–07	2100–08
Teacher #3	4100–08	4100–09	Dept. Mtg.	4522–04	Lunch	S 4617–01	Plan	4811–06	4811–07
Teacher #4	6800–06	D 6262–01	Plan	D 6365–01	6400–04	Lunch	D 6365–02	D 6262–02	Dept. Mtg.
Teacher #5	D 7902–01	Plan	D 7901–01	7476–05	Lunch	D 7902–02	7476–06	Dept. Mtg.	D 7901–02

Table 8.26 Enter Remainder of Courses: Day 1/Day 2 or Semester 1/Semester 2

Period	A1	A2	A3	A4		B1	B2	B3	B4
Teacher #1	S 1015– 01	S 1900– 01	DM/ Plan	1013– 04		TM/ Plan	1013– 05	1013– 06	1013– 07
Teacher #2	2100– 05	2100– 06	TM/ Plan	S 2105– 01		S 2107– 01	DM/ Plan	2100– 07	2100– 08
Teacher #3	DM/ Plan	4100– 08	4100– 09	4811– 06		4100– 10	S 4617– 01	TM/ Plan	4811– 07
Teacher #4	6800– 06	D 6262– 01	TM/ Plan	D 6365– 01		6800– 07	D 6365– 02	D 6262– 02	DM/ Plan
Teacher #5	D 7902– 01	DM/ Plan	D 7901– 01	7476– 07		D 7902– 02	TM/ Plan	7476– 08	D 7901– 02

Step 18: Initial and Subsequent Computer Runs

Once the prerequisite steps are completed, the stage is set for the first computer run. Prior to the run, encode the master schedule and enter student requests. Identify and determine weight of students with the greatest number of singletons and unique needs. Because these students are prone to having the most conflicts, run this partial schedule first. After the first run for all students, the computer identifies students with incomplete schedules as well as a list of sections that did not fill. Finding these challenges, modify the master schedule. Student requests, however, should not be altered.

Complete a second computer run once revisions are complete. Ideally, the percentage of students fully scheduled increases. Repeat this procedure until the greatest numbers of students are fully scheduled with their first choice courses. Following this conclusion, administrators

Table 8.27 Enter Remainder of Courses: Trimester

Teacher	Trimester #1					Trimester #2					Trimester #3				
	1	2	3	4	5	6	7	8	9	10	11	12	13	14	15
Teacher #1	AP Eng. 12A-01	Eng. 10A 01	Eng. 10A 02	Plan	H Eng. 11A-01	AP Eng. 12B-01	Eng. 10A 03	H Eng. 10A-01	Plan	H Eng. 11B-01	Eng. 10B 01	Plan	H Eng. 10B-01	Eng. 10B 02	Eng. 10B 03
Teacher #2	US 11A-01	Plan	AP US 11A-01	US 11A-02	US 11A-03	H SS 11A-01	US 11A-04	AP US 11B-01	H Govt. A-02	Plan	HSS 11B-01	H Govt. B-02	US 11B-01	US 11B-02	Plan
Teacher #3	Alg. II A-03	Alg. II A-04	Plan	Alg. II A-05	Alg. I A-01	H Alg. I A-01	Alg. II B-03	Plan	H Geo. A-01	Alg. I B-01	H Alg. I B-01	Alg. II B-04	Plan	H Geo. B-01	Alg. I C-01
Teacher #4	H Bio. A-01	Bio. A-01	Bio. A-02	Env. A-01	Plan	Bio. A-04	Bio. B-01	Env. B-01	Bio. B-02	Plan	Bio. B-03	Bio. B-04	H Bio-B-01	Plan	Env. A-06

and/or counselors meet with any students not fully scheduled to make necessary changes in course requests. In principle, 100% of students will have complete schedules for the first day of school.

Step 19: Implement Professional Development

Professional development sets the stage for teacher ownership as well as an effective and equitable schedule. All stakeholders need the understanding that the schedule is the means to a goal and not the end goal in itself. Most successful when implemented as an ongoing process, professional development content should include the purpose of college and career readiness, the role and function of small learning communities, interdisciplinary and single-subject team collaboration, RtI, the potential of an advisory/mentoring program, and teaching in extended-time periods.

Recap

Creating a high school schedule is a complex and detailed-oriented process. The final product creates a mechanism for students to receive course requests that reflect their needs, interests, and career aspirations. The steps in this chapter accomplish that goal consistent with the mission/vision statement and the resources available. The next chapter guides all constituency groups through a process to ensure success for the work completed in Chapters 5–8.

Points to Consider

1. How has the mission/vision statement guided the work in building the schedule?

2. In developing the schedule, how did the committee gain faculty understanding and support?

3. How does the schedule enable teachers to implement the three tiers of RtI?

4. Describe faculty involvement in selecting a primary framework and inserts.

5. How will the faculty contribute to developing houses, magnets, and academies?

6. Identify opportunities for collaboration in the schedule.

7. Assess how the schedule accommodates required and elective courses.

8. What efforts are made to avoid tracking?

9. How were teachers involved in decision-making?

10. In what ways does the schedule allow for flexibility?

11. How does the schedule meet the needs of a diverse population?

12. How does the schedule provide the least restrictive environment for all students?

13. How does the professional development program encourage teachers to take ownership of the schedule?

14. To what extent are schedules within the district consistent?

15. Were sufficient runs of the master schedule completed to ensure students' first choice of courses?

Aspects of Schedule Implementation

9

Focus

- Computer usage
- Establishing goals
- Professional development
- Common planning periods
- Lesson planning

As in the classroom, understanding emerges in performance. Indicated in the chapters on developing a schedule, the mission/vision statement guides both schedule building and instruction. An awareness of its importance lies in the schedule design and in teacher implementation of the tenets in the statements.

Once the human element of the schedule design is in place, the computer increases its role. Chapters 5–8 focus on the initial draft of a schedule based on student requests. Once firm, the draft is encoded into the computer software package adopted by the district. Following an initial run, an analysis is performed determining the completeness of student schedules and sections with remaining seats. Depending on the percentage of fully scheduled students, the master schedule may need modification and the analysis process repeated. Once the desired maximum percentage point is reached, the remaining unscheduled students may need to alter their choices. When all is complete, print the schedule.

Since implementation of the schedule is the shared responsibility of the superintendent, central office staff, principal, and teachers, each makes an individual commitment to the process. Examples of personal goals set by each to move toward implementation follow:

Superintendent

- Assess the distribution and equitable use of FTEs.
- Inform board of education and community about the schedule's reflection of the mission/vision statements.
- Visit schools to observe actualization of special programs.

Central Office Staff

- Offer support during teacher observation and evaluation sessions.
- Visit schools to reinforce actualization of special programs.

Principal

- Accept leadership role in motivating staff to implement schedule.
- Offer continued informal assessment during classroom observations and walk-through visits.

Teachers

- Use time effectively in developing lessons.
- Capitalize on opportunities for flexibility.
- Contribute to opportunities for collaboration.

Perhaps the most significant aspect of implementation, professional development for the staff determines the ultimate success of the schedule. Three areas comprise this phase: intervention, collaboration, and use of instructional time.

In order for the intervention program to have fluidity and adequate implementation, it requires understanding by all. The responsibility for its success depends on team collaboration for the coordination and assessment of the program.

The assumption that all persons involved know and understand how to function as a collaborating unit is a common misunderstanding. In order for teams, cohorts, magnets, houses, and academies at all educational levels to function, members need to have an established understanding of collaboration and its purpose in an educational setting. With this understanding, team members know what should occur during planning time as well as other opportunities for collaboration. Without efficient use of the common planning time period, valuable educational and instructional discussion is lost. One way to determine the cohesiveness and understanding of collaborative time is to use the self-evaluation instrument in Table 9.1. This instrument can be completed individually and discussed as a group, completed as a group, and, if desired after group discussion, discussed in part or whole with an administrator.

Table 9.1 Collaboration Time Assessment Instrument

Question	Consistently	Frequently	Occasionally	Comments
Do team members address student needs?				
Does the team use data in making decisions?				
Do team members reflect upon the mission/vision statement?				
Do team members explore their commitment to students and colleagues?				
Do team members utilize the potential of resource personnel?				

Continued

Question	Consistently	Frequently	Occasionally	Comments
Are leadership responsibilities shared?				
Do team members participate equally in decision-making?				
Are guidelines for gaining consensus followed?				
Are team decisions implemented?				
Are records kept of team decisions?				
Do team members integrate content and skills?				
Are teachers not on the team informed of key decisions?				
Do team members recognize the relationship between planning periods and the instructional program?				
Do team members recognize the relationship between planning periods and the intervention program?				

Continued

Table 9.1 Continued

Question	Consistently	Frequently	Occasionally	Comments
Are parents involved in the team process?				
Do team members discuss appropriate teaching strategies?				
Do team members make use of flexible time opportunities?				
Do team members offer suggestions for the design of the master schedule?				
Does the team have an agenda for all meetings?				
Do team members utilize opportunities to group and regroup students for instructional purposes?				
Do department meetings focus on vertical alignment?				
Do subject-area teachers implement existing curriculum?				

Continued

Question	Consistently	Frequently	Occasionally	Comments
Do subject-area teachers offer suggestions for curriculum revision?				

The schedule exists as a tool for delivery of instruction. Within each period, bell-to-bell instruction leads toward academic achievement. By applying understanding of how people learn and use time within the class period, instructional delivery capitalizes on the time allocated in the schedule. People learn through a conceptual lens that connects experiences, knowledge, and patterns.

In the daily lesson, learning goals move the student toward assimilation and adaptation of information through a series of sequential, articulated engagements in which the student is actively involved. Recall and rehearsal reinforce the learning while positive feedback gives students necessary information to move forward. Reflection time for students needs to be built into the lesson, and reflection time for teachers needs to be built into their professional day. Ongoing assessment of student learning takes place throughout the lesson just as ongoing assessment of teacher use of instructional time takes place throughout the year. Each of the above elements of a lesson contributes to enhancing student achievement through the efficient use of available time within the schedule.

Recap

A relationship exists between school organization, schedule implementation, and supervision of the instructional program. Administrators and instructional supervisors use that relationship in walk-through visits and the classroom observation process including preconference, actual classroom visits, and post-observation sessions to accomplish the goal of the schedule.

Points to Consider

1. How does the mission/vision statement guide the implementation of the schedule?

2. Have stakeholders established goals that focus on meaningful implementation?

3. To what extent is the master schedule effective in scheduling students' first choice of courses?

4. To what extent have teachers received continuing professional development on collaboration?

5. Do teachers use the self-evaluation instrument efficiently?

6. To what extent is ongoing professional development in place for bell-to-bell instruction?

7. In what ways are all stakeholders engaged in school organization, schedule implementation, and supervision of the instructional program?